TO ORDER ADDITIONAL BOOKS IN THE SERIES

EDUCATED INVESTING

PLEASE CONTACT PALISADE BUSINESS PRESS

WWW.PALBIZPRESS.COM

FOR ADDITIONAL CONTACT INFORMATION
SEE BELOW OR BACK OF BOOK

PORTIONS OF THIS BOOK — INCLUDING ITS MAJOR ANALYTICAL CORE PROVIDED BY PALISADE BUSINESS PRESS — APPEAR IN OTHER BOOKS IN THIS SERIES AND ELSEWHERE IN OTHER FORMS.

AF864872

Palisade Business Press is a division of Palisade Press Inc.

ZHANGS ON EDUCATED INVESTING Published by PBP. Printed in the United States of America. For information write to Palisade Press, PO Box 8358, Jersey City, New Jersey 07308-8358. Checks should be made payable to Palisade Press.

PRINTED IN THE UNITED STATES OF AMERICA
A SPECIAL LIMITED EDITION
ISBN: 1-893958-16-7

AUTHORS' BIOS

CHARLES C. ZHANG

Charles C. Zhang, CFP, ChFC, CLU, CMFC, MBA is founder of the financial firm Zhang & Associates and is affiliated with a leading national, financial service company.

Mr. Zhang is the #1 rated financial advisor out of the company's 8,900 financial advisors nationwide. He is also named as one of the five "ACE Advisors," the nation's most innovative and successful financial professionals, in 1998 by *Ticker* magazine. He has received the designation of "DALBAR Rated Financial Professional, 1998," from the nation's only financial advisor rating program.

Mr. Zhang holds some of the most prestigious professional designations and degrees in the financial planning field. He is a Certified Financial Planner® (CFP®) Professional, a Chartered Financial Consultant (ChFC), a Chartered Life Underwriter (CLU) and a Chartered Mutual Fund Consultant (CMFC). He has an MBA degree and a Master of Arts in Economics degree. Mr. Zhang has been cited on financial issues in several national publications. He is an adjunct professor in the Department of Finance and Commercial Law at Western Michigan University and also an approved adjunct faculty member for the College for Financial Planning.

LYNN CHEN-ZHANG

Lynn Chen-Zhang, CPA, serves as Director for Client Service at Zhang & Associates. She is a Certified Public Accountant (CPA) and has a Master of Science in Accountancy. Prior to joining her husband's firm, she was a senior tax consultant for one of the top five CPA firms and a tax manager for one of the Fortune 500 companies.

THE ZHANGS ON EDUCATED INVESTING

A SPECIAL LIMITED EDITION

PUBLISHED BY

PALISADE BUSINESS PRESS

PBP

PALISADE PRESS PO BOX 8358
JERSEY CITY, NEW JERSEY 07308-8358
Nation's Leading Cooperative Publisher

PUBLISHER'S NOTE

Welcome to Palisade Press' special limited edition series, *On Educated Investing*. We are proud to present this book to you featuring investment advisors Charles and Lynn Zhang. Their stated allegiance to the concepts of financial planning and dedication to appropriate asset allocation techniques qualify them to be among the authors who participate with us in bringing this series to readers who want to understand more about investing.

HOW THE SERIES WORKS

Palisade Press' "core book" — constituting this work's major analytical core — is offered on a paid basis to top advisors and financial entrepreneurs who wish to express their own investment perspective and opinions alongside recognized approaches to diversified investing using appropriate asset allocation techniques. While the core book appears throughout the series, Palisade Press is selective about the advisors with whom it works and attempts to ascertain that participants subscribe to the theories espoused in the core book. The core book is often customized in consultation with the advisor.

DISTRIBUTION

Books in Palisade Press' series, *On Educated Investing*, are available directly from Palisade Press, from the participating author-advisor, from local bookstores in the advisor's area — and over the Internet, as well at **WWW.PALBIZPRESS.COM.** For information write to Palisade Press, PO Box 8358, Jersey City, New Jersey 07308-8358.

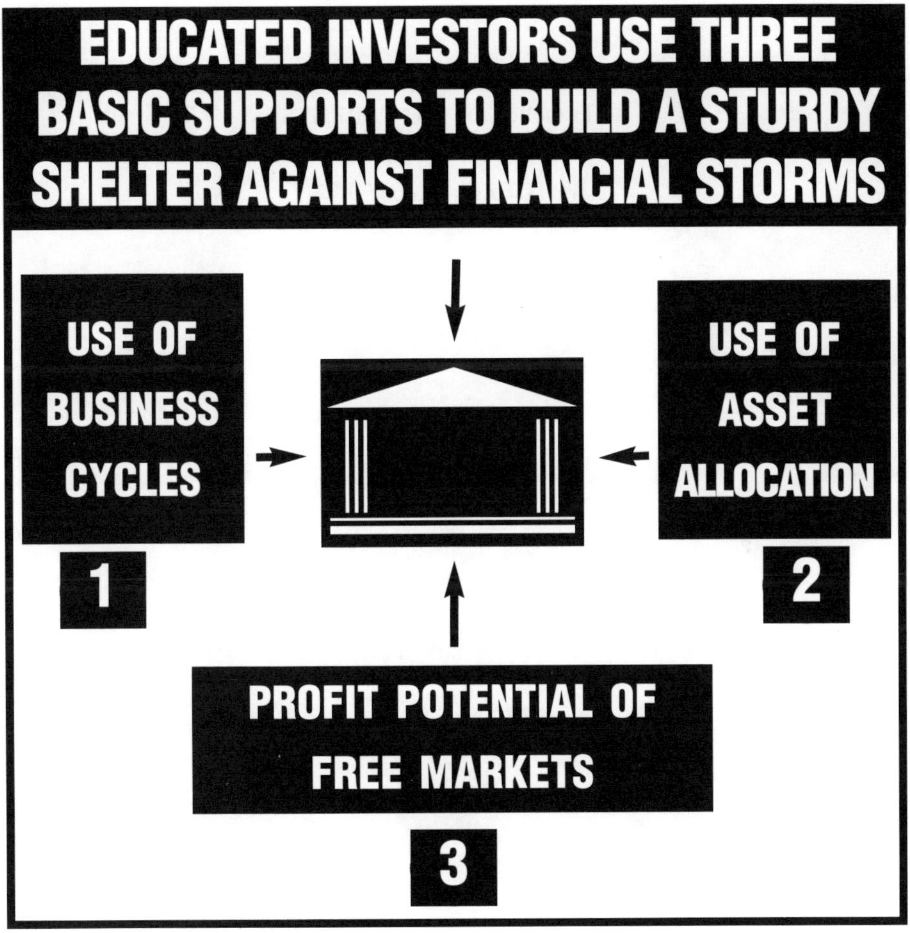
EDUCATED INVESTORS USE THREE BASIC SUPPORTS TO BUILD A STURDY SHELTER AGAINST FINANCIAL STORMS
USE OF BUSINESS CYCLES
1
USE OF ASSET ALLOCATION
2
PROFIT POTENTIAL OF FREE MARKETS
3

To our loving parents
and beautiful children,
Mitchell and Alex

TABLE OF CONTENTS

ONE: INVESTMENT PRINCIPLES

TWO: UNDERSTANDING INVESTMENT ISSUES

FOUR: 21ST CENTURY INVESTING

ONE

INVESTMENT PRINCIPLES

1

EDUCATED INVESTING

WHERE WE'RE GOING
HOW TO GET THERE

Hello, we're the Zhangs — Charles and Lynn Zhang.

We're pleased to participate in this series of books about Educated Investing.

As we look toward the 21st century, we're sure many readers, as well as many of our clients, will agree that there is little that is more critical in their lives than understanding the power of our modern economic system. We all want to put it to work for our advantage — while protecting ourselves as much as possible from its excesses.

Educated Investors understand the miracle of our modern capitalist system and the powerful mechanism that increasingly drives prosperity and profitability throughout the world. Educated Investors are appreciative of the way this mechanism enables them to invest and profit from the imagination and hard work of others.

But Educated Investors are also well aware that such a broad and powerful system, encompassing so many possibilities, is also complex and demands a good deal of attention.

Not everyone is — or can be — an Educated Investor. It's not something that happens without hard work and concentration. Most people we would call Educated Investors only get there because they have done a great deal of reading and thinking about the modern investment process. To be a truly Educated Investor in this sense means to have absorbed a good deal of information about the evolution of economic history, as well as political history and the more arcane information about the evolution of our domestic financial industry — perhaps the most powerful in the world.

But maybe it doesn't have to be quite so complicated as all that. After all, information and education often resolve themselves into fairly simple conclusions. The trouble is getting to those conclusions with a comfortable degree of certainty.

You may not feel certain about our conclusions, but this book should provide you with some of the basics of Educated Investing — basics that might otherwise take you a very long time to acquire and internalize.

If you are a reader not commonly exposed to this kind of information, we feel a little envious. We wish we'd read this kind of book when we were starting out. We would have saved a lot of searching.

Think of this book, then, as a beginning. After all, that's what Educated Investing is all about. It's a process, not an end result. It's a state of being, a destination you may never arrive at.

If that's sounds slightly mystical, well maybe it is. Markets are the result of billions of sophisticated buying and selling decisions. We can make reasonable recommendations based on reasonable assumptions, but we'll never know it all. Anyone who tells you that he or she does know it all is a fool. Run, don't

Markets are the result of billions of sophisticated buying and selling decisions. We can make reasonable recommendations based on reasonable assumptions, but we'll never know it all.

walk, the other way.

Historical indices can give us an idea of certain basic patterns — and Educated Investors are aware of them. Stocks' aggregate returns, for instance, are higher than those of bonds. Certainly that has been the case in the 1980s and 1990s as Baby Boomers continue to save for retirement using equities as the preferred store of value.

But let's think about the process of becoming an Educated Investor another way. Let's examine what it does not mean:

- An Educated Investor is not necessarily someone who reads investment magazines and watches shows about money.
- An Educated Investor does not necessarily understand accounting or investment terminology.
- An Educated Investor does not necessarily spend a good deal of time minding his or her investments.

Instead, being an Educated Investor means understanding at a fundamental level how money works. It is important for an Educated Investor to understand the elements that make up investing, instruments such as stocks and bonds, and the blending of these elements into various products such as funds and partnerships. But by understanding, at a fundamental level what money is, how business cycles occur and the impact that these cycles have on investing, Educated Investors are able to predict, not follow, trends.

Becoming an Educated Investor is hard work. But the benefits — control of your life and an understanding of how the economy works, and your situation in it — make the effort worthwhile.

A frame of reference is an invaluable thing. Knowledge is power. And power generates control over money, over the direction of your life, over your family's happiness as your kids grow up and you shape the direction of your own life to gain maximum happiness and success.

ZHANGS ON EDUCATED INVESTING

As we've moved forward with our careers, we've been careful to take the time to educate ourselves about money — how it's made, who makes it and where it goes. Now we're happy to pass this information on to you.

2
OUR STORY

HOW WE LEARNED ABOUT INVESTING AND WHY WE BECAME FINANCIAL ADVISORS

My wife and I believe in hard work — when it comes to our careers and, more importantly, when it comes to insuring that our clients' portfolios are appropriately positioned to do as well as possible no matter what the financial climate.

Hard work is perhaps the number one factor in successful investing — but many people misunderstand the nature of the "hard work" that planners, advisors and clients need to do. Everyone involved in successful — Educated — investing must perform the hard work of sticking with market ups and downs rather than trying to time the market. They also need to discipline themselves when it comes to their expectations. People who want to invest for potential higher returns must realize that they will be taking more risk than they may be comfortable with. An investor who does not discipline his or her expectations is an investor who will probably experience a good amount of frustration over the market's long-term.

My wife, Lynn, and I make it our jobs to help clients avoid this type of frustration by educating them about the risk and returns of investing.

When we set off on this journey, we didn't plan on building this kind of financial business together — at least not right away. After receiving my Master's Degree in Economics from Western Michigan University, I became affiliated with a leading, national financial advisory firm while Lynn continued in graduate school. Because of that, I decided to build my practice, Charles Zhang & Associates, in the Kalamazoo and Battle Creek area so that I could stay near her.

Eventually Lynn was able to find a job with Price Waterhouse as a tax consultant and later became a Certified Public Accountant (CPA). After Price Waterhouse, she joined Kellogg, a Fortune 500 company, as a tax manager.

Lynn was able to gain good experience at these corporations, but often told me that she felt frustrated because she didn't see the result of all of her hard work. So, it became more apparent that it was time for her to join me at the practice. Then all of her hard work became more meaningful.

When I started my career, one of my very early clients was a professor of mine — and I was very pleased with his vote of confidence. I must admit though that I had a tough time for the first six months. I didn't have any experience in marketing and I soon discovered that marketing is the key to success. If you cannot find clients, you'll never have a chance to prove your worth or provide value.

I used to work 80 or 90 hours a week, trying to figure out how to get my name out there. Gradually, as it usually does, hard work paid off in the end.

I was able to begin working with clients, investing their funds, and educating them about diversification and long-

We want to be a leading financial planning firm, and to this end we need to keep up with our knowledge, take additional courses and continue to learn as best we can.

term investment goals. My business was beginning to take shape. More importantly, acquiring assets under management gave me the ability to begin to purse my profession in a creative and dedicated way.

Today, because of my success, we are able to put on a couple of seminars each year for our clients and prospects. We are able to bring in guest speakers from different mutual fund and real estate companies to provide another perspective as it relates to financial planning, retirement and estate planning.

The key, I find, is to be honest with your clients. People can truly tell when someone is just telling them something in order to make a sale. I think by following that one piece of advice I have been able to gain the trust of my clients and in return they give me referrals. Word of mouth is the best kind of marketing.

In 1993, I became a Gold Team planner, which ranked me in the top 10% of the national planning firm with which I was affiliated. In my fourth year, I became a President's Advisory Council (PAC) member — in recognition of placing in the top 1% of advisors. In my fifth year, I became the number one producer out of the company's 8,900 financial advisors nationwide.

I became a President's Advisor Council (PAC) member — in recognition of placing in the top 1% of advisors. I also became the firm's number one financial advisor in terms of assets gathered. In 1988, I was named one of five "Ace" advisors.

In 1998, I had the honor of being chosen as one of five "Ace" advisors, the nation's most successful and innovative financial professionals, by *Ticker* magazine, a national, professional investment magazine. By this time, Lynn had joined the business.

Lynn and I place great value on sincerity and service. We always keep our promises, and we follow up right away. Today, we work with about 600 clients and we want to continue to grow in a controlled manner, accumulating around 80 clients per year who are serious about the financial planning process.

We currently have over $200 million under management — much invested in wrap fee accounts that have domestic and international exposure. Our clients have the choice to either work on a fee basis or commission basis, but most prefer fee only.

Ever since the beginning, we have strongly believed in the asset allocation approach — spreading a client's investments among a mix of investment classes to increase potential reward while decreasing risk. We tend to use a combination of both passive and active management when working with our clients. In order to track the performance of our clients' portfolios, we use Morningstar research as well as some internal software that we have created to measure risk and return. It's very important to have the technology to track these investments since we offer 2,900 mutual funds from 250 different mutual fund families among our asset allocation choices.

Our goal is to find strategies that lower risk while maximizing the potential return of profit. Asset allocation gives us tools to help the client lower risk and raise return by investing in many markets and asset classes around the world. Institutional investors use asset allocation techniques to determine the amount of risk they wish to tolerate, the return they want to achieve and the international blend of assets that can most efficiently assist them in reaching their goals.

Once we've set up an allocation plan with clients, we review performance regularly. Preparation for each service appointment is quite time consuming so I have had to hire four assistants. Two of them are fully licensed to do necessary trading; the other two perform support work. While Lynn and I continue to live in Kalamazoo, we also have offices in both Battle Creek and Grand Rapids as well.

We are on our way to becoming a leading financial planning firm, and we understand the need for continuing education. Additionally, I serve as a part-time professor for Western Michigan University in the finance department.

Our vision has always been to have people in our community think of Charles Zhang & Assoc. when they think of financial planning.

3

PLANNING AHEAD

THE EDUCATED INVESTOR PLANS AHEAD — AND DOES SO FOR LIFE

The Educated Investor plans ahead — and does so for life. The older investor must husband financial resources; the younger must create those resources. The American worker retires on government benefits (Social Security and Medicare), employee benefits, personal savings and investments. With retirement comes decisions about supplemental medical coverage, pension distribution and actual retirement age. According to the U.S. Bureau of Labor Statistics the average worker in 1900 spent less than two years in retirement. Today that average is more than 16 years. The more years spent in retirement, the more income needed.

In this chapter we will examine, generally, the arsenal available to American savers who wish to prepare themselves as best they can for a secure old age and active retirement.

Social Security: Social Security is perhaps the most widely known American "retirement" plan, set up in the Franklin Delano Roosevelt years to insure that every citizen would prepare for his or her age by contributing to a pay-as-you-go retirement fund which the government would organize and safeguard. Today, there is much talk about Social Security "going broke" because the group of workers paying into the fund is gradually diminishing while the group of workers retiring and taking money out the fund is growing.

A number of plans have been suggested to reverse the demographic difficulties of Social Security. Among them are more aggressive investments in securities other than those of the short-term fixed-income nature with which the fund is currently involved. Democrats have even urged that government itself invest Social Security funds in the larger marketplace, specifically the stock market. Republicans, concerned with the idea that government itself would invade the private sector with a massive investment pool, have suggested that individuals be given the right to invest their Social Security funds as they fit in a variety of instruments including stocks. While this debate is ongoing, the reality remains that Social Security — as successful as it has been in the middle- to late-20th century — is currently a program in trouble, one that today's Educated Investors may count on to secure only a portion of their retirement, if that.

The Educated Investor must look to other investments — those within his or her control — in order to wisely allocate financial resources and plan carefully for his or her retirement.

Yet, nationwide, spending is up and saving is down. Life expectancy keeps increasing while taxes and inflation eat into retirement funds. A well-thought out financial plan is crucial. How does the Educated Investor go about it?

Planning means setting goals in financial matters as in other matters. Age influences decisions. Younger workers may focus on home ownership and vacation plans while grandparents may look to finance the education of grandchildren.

The Personal Financial Plan: Planning means setting goals in financial matters as in other matters. Age influences decisions. Younger workers may focus on home ownership and vacation plans while grandparents may look to finance the education of grandchildren. Still, each personal financial plan must answer basic money questions such as current financial status, resources needed for goals, and develop a timeline for arriving at goals and ways to reach those goals. Let's examine some of the tools available to the Educated Investor when it comes to building a personal financial plan.

Disciplined Savings: Accumulating wealth by systematic financial initiatives triggered by disciplined, personal goals is the way American workers must prepare for retirement. Business- and income-producing property and a well-designed investment portfolio may be parts of this picture. Managing both debt and taxes are vital issues for such planning.

Most financial advisors cannot emphasize saving enough. Authorizing bank or credit union transfer of a fixed amount to savings each month is a significant step. The investing of a large sum one may acquire into a money market or short-term bond account is another significant step. Increasing one's saving rate yearly is a hedge against inflation later.

Cash: A personal financial plan begins with establishing net worth, both current and projected. Spending minus income equals disposable income — and it is disposable income one uses to increase wealth though saving and investing.

Experts often say that a financial plan should have three- to six-months' living expenses in cash reserve as so-called liquid assets. What this means is that this amount can be turned into cash immediately if needed. A sensible financial plan has cash reserves that are available readily or assets easily converted into cash should need arise. Remember to consider present security and future well-being in setting financial goals and deciding how to meet those goals.

Checking accounts, savings accounts, short-term certificates of deposit and money market funds are liquid assets. Certain liquid assets are suitable for a process called laddering. Certificates of deposit, money market accounts and bonds which have fixed maturity rates can be structured to come due at regular intervals thus earning higher interest and dividends, but yet being available without penalty if needed.

Securities: Once the Educated Investor has established his

TERMS YOU SHOULD KNOW

CLOSED-END FUND: a fund, typically listed on an exchange, often composed of securities, whose total value is more than the actual price at which the fund's shares are trading. Since closed-end fund managers have no obligation to redeem shares at net asset value, fund participants are often forced to sell for less than their shares are actually worth.

COMMODITY: goods of a non-financial nature such as grain or metals, often traded on a futures exchange.

DEBT: longer-term fixed income securities.

DERIVATIVE(S): securities whose worth is based on an underlying instrument. Prices of options and financial futures, for instance, have some connection to the movements of underlying equity. But many derivatives are traded off-exchange; their popularity is growing along with questions about how well Wall Street actually understands the risks inherent in these OTC customized instruments.

EQUITY: in industry terminology, a fancy word for stocks.

EXCHANGE: used to be a building, owned or rented by members, where securities were traded. Now can refer to an electronic net.

FINANCIAL FUTURE: futures contract including those based on underlying instruments such as long bonds, mortgages or stock indexes.

HEDGE FUND: Secretive firms using sophisticated financial investing techniques, often in several markets, and primarily concerned with proprietary trading profit rather than agency business.

INDEX: a large group of securities, supposedly with similar charac-

or her personal financial plan, focused on necessary cash reserves, and set up a disciplined savings approach, contributions can be invested each month in a variety of securities using a variety of investment strategies.

Because there is so much need for investing, it has naturally attracted the attention and energies of many motivated financial executives — each of whom is busy trying to come up with a tempting product or array of products that will gather investors' cashflows. Before investors consider what instruments in which to place their savings, they must contend with the types of investments available — from fixed and variable annuities to mutual funds, futures pools, hedge funds, "wrap fee" programs, Real Estate Investments Trusts,

TERMS YOU SHOULD KNOW

teristics, tracked as a group.

INITIAL PUBLIC OFFERING (IPO): the first offering of stock to the public.

LIMITED PARTNERSHIP: these come in two flavors, public and private. Private partnerships are restricted to 100 partners or less, along with a general partner or partners; public partnerships may have thousands of investors, usually at $5,000 per, along with a general partner or partners.

MUTUAL FUND: these are funds, open or closed-end, that operate under the rules of the 1940 Investment Company Act, which mandates disclosure of performance and investment objectives.

OPTION: the ability or right to purchase a financial instrument at a certain time for a certain price. If the ability is not exercised, it lapses.

REAL ESTATE INVESTMENT TRUSTS (REITS): a company overseeing a real estate portfolio for shareholders and passing along profits, if any.

SECURITY(IES): bonds, stocks, other kinds of financial instruments, offered publicly or privately.

STOCK: ownership in a corporation.

TREASURY (TREASURYS): government bonds.

UNDERWRITING: the process of purchasing securities from an issuer with the intent of selling them soon; a function commonly performed by Wall Street's banking firms.

limited partnerships — the list goes on and on.

These investment types are, of course, only tools that help the investor realize his or her savings goals. In order to use them, the Educated Investor must discern his or her realistic savings goals, the kind of retirement that is wished for and the amount of risk that he or she can cope with on a regular basis. Risk, as we shall see, is nothing more than volatility over time. However, this innocent-sounding phrase has caused as much agitation and heartache as the war between the sexes and other historical and ongoing human difficulties. While it may be comforting to know that one's investments may return to their previous level of profitability after moving down quickly, this knowledge may seem uncomfortably theoretical to someone facing college bills or a looming balloon-mortgage payment.

The Educated Investor therefore will take a careful look at his or her financial situation, bearing in mind how much volatility is emotionally sustainable. Investments will be placed accordingly — with the realization that equities are ordinarily the most volatile of investments, while fixed-income and other debt instruments, when appropriately backed, are less tension inducing because they guarantee return of principal at the end of a fixed period.

Fixed assets grow at predictable rates while equity assets accumulate wealth at a faster rate but with greater risk. Balancing the individual portfolio is called asset allocation. A well developed body of data on historical trends which financial advisors have at their fingertips helps the investor balance a portfolio.

Low-risk, low-return investments include certificates of deposit, treasury securities and bonds, fixed annuities and of course checking and savings accounts. Bonds and trusts yield higher profits and may have tax advantages. Mutual funds, corporate bonds and investment trusts move up the scale of higher risk, higher return through common stock, speculative stock, real estate and collectibles.

Insurance: Even if one is a risk-taker when it comes to investments, he or she will admit that a vital aspect of the personal financial plan is protection of what one already has. A primary concern is providing for dependents in case of death or disability of the wage earner. Auto, home and personal liability protection require attention as does consideration of mortgage protection. Health care costs and possible long-term care costs are immediate considerations, particularly for older workers and those already retired.

Home ownership: This is the major financial asset of most Americans, an equity asset whose market value may go up or dow. Like the stock market itself, real estate is a fairly variable investment, subject to regular highs and lows. Many investors remember the hot market of the 1980s, which peaked somewhere around the stock market crash of '87. Similarly, real estate enjoyed a boom in the late 1990s, with many regions of the country experiencing another "hot" market that raised demand without a similar increase in home mortgages offered by financial institutions.

Educated Investors may choose to invest in real estate in a disciplined way through Real Estate Investment Trusts (Reits) and other liquid, fund-like approaches. Others may simply purchase real estate outright, bearing in mind that the market is variable and often mirrors the cycles of the larger economy — heating up when the markets themselves are enjoying good times and diminishing in a recessionary climate. Additionally, real estate is not a very liquid investments and thus the Educated Investor will make sure that he or she is solvent enough to allow liquidation at his or her choice — not at "firesale prices" because of financial need.

In this chapter, we have seen that a personal financial plan calls for a disciplined perspective on one's future needs, an understanding of one's tolerance for risk, and a comprehension of the different kinds of available investments at home and around the world. No wonder many who start down the path to building their own financial plans decide they require the assistance of a financial advisor.

4
GETTING HELP

HOW TO CHOOSE A FINANCIAL ADVISOR TO HELP WITH THE PLANNING PROCESS

We have seen that the Educated Investor building a solid financial plan has much to consider in the way of investment options. With all the complexity involved, investors may well wish to have help.

But how does one go about choosing a financial advisor to help with the planning process? Here are some points to consider.

Look closely at the credentials of prospective financial advisors. Remember, certified financial planners pass a rigorous examination covering tax, retirement and estate planning as well as employee benefits, investment and insurance management.

Get recommendations. Friends, acquaintances, even family members may have valuable information about planners and their services. A first-hand recommendation can be a valuable tool in the creation of a "short list" of prospective advisors.

Ask the potential financial advisor all sorts of questions. Ask for a sample financial plan and inquire about the planner's experience: Does this planner work with other professionals such as brokers and insurance agents? Will this planner refer you for more complex issues to experts such as attorneys and accountants?

Understand the planner's fee system before beginning a financial relationship. Is this planner paid a salary, an hourly rate, a flat rate or a percentage of assets invested?

Ask for estimates of fees. As part of this fee-evaluation, assess the reputation of a prospective financial advisor. Any disciplinary action of registered representatives and of securities investment organizations can be found by calling the NASD Regulations Public Disclosure Hotline.

How the Planner Can Help

Times have changed and therefore traditional retirement has changed. When we retire now, we live longer and are in better health. More wealth is needed to do the things retirees want to do. Some people plan ahead and put away large sums. Others have less with which to invest. Many retirees opt to keep working but may change occupations.

Determining Priorities. Certainly individuals vary greatly in the amount of risk they want to take with their money. This is an important factor when putting together the investment portfolio. Learning all one can about one's own business is an important way to ease anxiety. Being in control of one's finances is a good feeling.

In this consumer-oriented era, most Americans spend more than they earn. How then can they invest? Only by self discipline. Begin by determining what is most important in a financial sense. Set priorities. These might include a new home, educating children, a comfortable retirement, being in control of one's financial affairs. Saving to invest and investing to save are integral parts of an overall financial plan derived from setting financial goals and sticking to them.

Determining Cash Flow. Determining cash flow or what one spends and how one spends it precedes saving to invest. Acquiring the habit of not spending all one earns is difficult. After analysis of spending habits, choices can be made of what is most important. What can a person do without and what spending is necessary? Which expenditure is based on need and which on desire?

Often a simple and painless way to save is automatic payroll withdrawal by one's employer. A system of bank authorization is the next best to payroll deduction. An unexpected amount of cash or income can boost the savings and investment of an investor dramatically if it is put into the portfolio rather than spent especially for goods that depreciate (a car) or services (eating out) which have no rate of return.

Determining Investment Types. Resolving to save to invest brings more choices to the would-be investor. Some investments have tax advantages. Others do not. Knowing the difference adds flexibility to a portfolio and increases wealth. Taxes deferred until retirement are taxed at a lower rate, usually because the tax bracket becomes lower.

Determining Strategies. The new investor is advised to invest with dollar-cost averaging as the mechanism. This is simply investing the same amount at regular intervals. The market as a whole moves in a generally upward direction so investment increases wealth progressively. When the price is low more shares are bought and when the price is high fewer shares are bought with the same amount of investment.

The value of a stock can drop. The market itself can fail. A particular segment of the market can drop. Interest rates may vary affecting markets particularly bond markets. However over the long run the range of volatility in a well-balanced portfolio is narrow thus perseverance is rewarded. In a diversified portfolio no one investment is paramount so one failure or decrease does not create a crisis for the investor. A prudent investor neither kills or gets killed in the market.

All investors want the highest rate of return at the least possible risk. The old saw of not putting all of one's eggs in one basket is an apt analogy. A dropped basket breaks all the eggs in it, while the eggs in another basket are saved.

Stocks, bonds, annuities, securities, real-estate. What is the right mix? The answer to that question goes to financial goals and assets available to achieve those goals.

5

DOS AND DON'TS

WHAT A GOOD FINANCIAL ADVISOR WILL POINT OUT TO A SINCERE AND MOTIVATED INVESTOR

The end of the Cold War and the growing market economy around the world presents new opportunities in international investing. What will a good financial advisor point out to a sincere and motivated investor? Here are some points that we make to our clients. (Perhaps we've mentioned some of these before, but there's no harm in a little repetition.)

Do use dollar-cost averaging. Don't put one large sum in one market. Put the same amount in at regular intervals. Mutual funds are a good idea. Do diversify the investment portfolio. Not too much in any one investment protects against strong fluctuation in a particular one. Short-term bonds earn less. Long-term bonds earn more but need to be carefully structured to mature in increments. Mutual funds are good vehicles for dollar-cost averaging. They grow in value with steady dividends. Do get invested. Stay invested and diversify investments.

Become familiar with terminology. One way to understand investment opportunities is to categorize them. Memorize terms such as "equity" and "debt" and try to lay them out mentally in a way that makes them useful as investment tools. Thus an Educated Investor thinking of "debt" might categorize debt as follows: government, municipal, corporate and "junk" (low-rated corporate debt) — instruments that move from "least risky" to "most risky" when it comes to fixed income investing.

Look ahead and plan to lessen taxes, allowing more finan-

cial resources for investing. Here perhaps the assistance of financial advisors is most necessary. Tax benefits and retirement plans change with new Federal laws, often with the yearly Federal budget. State laws involving inheritance and estate taxes may be impacted significantly by careful planning. Financial advisors keep up with changes in Federal and state laws and what those changes mean to their clients.

Changing jobs often means making decisions about retirement savings in accounts with employers. Choices may be complex: IRA; Roth IRA; cash distribution or retention in a company retirement plan.

Prepare for retirement well in advance. Retirement is an emotional transition as well as a financial one. Goals make transitions easier and, through planning, one is happier with decisions one must make. This is especially true in retirement. Things go better if there is a plan. The actual act of retiring returns the individual to the earlier process of goal setting, asset analysis and decision making.

There is no denying that retirement is more complicated than it used to be. Years ago when workers stayed with a single employer most of their working lives, companies provided a gold watch and a pension — no questions asked. Today, the questions are many. At retirement, workers are faced with decisions about what to do with large, still-untaxed sums. If the employer has both contributed to and invested in the retirement fund (perhaps a mutual fund) wisely, prudently and with luck, fortunate is the retiree. Too often, the retiree is not so fortunate. Mergers and acquisitions may eliminate benefits, and sometimes the

If the employer has both contributed to and invested in the retirement fund (perhaps a mutual fund) wisely, prudently and with luck, fortunate is the retiree.

potential retiree's job. Companies under bottom-line pressure — and what company is not these days — may be tempted to sack older employees first because of the expense of providing all those benefits. For these reasons, the Educated Investor will take special care to invest as much as possible on his or her own and will also closely track any non-corporate benefits to which he or she is entitled.

Pay careful attention to Social Security benefits and how you intend to take them. Social Security benefits can start at age 62 but there's a penalty for beginning the program before age 65. There is also a permanent reward for waiting till 70 years to receive benefits, in that the government will reward you with greater cash flow. Educated Investors would do well to sit down with a planner to determine when they wish to tap their benefits, taking into account their age, health and financial need. Another wrinkle to consider: Social Security benefits can be cut if earnings are too high after retirement; however, after age 70 there are no limits on how much a retiree may earn

Prepare for health care as well. Consideration of Social Security would not be complete without discussing health care following retirement. Except for certain pensions set by law, everyone gets Medicare after age 65 upon application for it even if retirement is delayed until 70. Medicare comes in two parts, A and B. Part A is free. Part B is deducted from Social Security benefits upfront. Everyone pays the same price and there are no costs for pre-existing conditions. Medicare with Part B covers many of the health care costs of retirees. Glaring omissions are prescriptions and long-term care in nursing homes. Horror stories abound of retirees who cannot afford the costly medications their physicians prescribe for them. Many estates are gutted and children and grandchildren left without inheritances when a parent or parents spend their last years in nursing homes. Supplementary insurance coverage and long-term care insurance are priorities in any financial plan.When shopping for supplemental health care policies, ask the following questions and get clear answers to them: Can the insurer cancel your policy?

Are there cost of living increases in the coverage? What are the time or money limits? Is home health care an option? Under certain conditions, the cost of long term care insurance is tax deductible.

Remembering the following facts will motivate you to plan for health care in advance just as you would for your retirement:

—Medicare *does not cover* home health care; long-term care; rehabilitation; prescriptions or medical care outside the U.S.

—Only 2-5% of long-term care costs are paid by Medicare. Those who need such care are those who pay for that care as a rule.

—The Health Insurance Association of America projects that four in ten Americans now over the age of 65 will need nursing home care.

—Typically the financial drain of long-term care comes at the end of life when taxes and inflation have taken a toll on fixed income.

—Private long-term care insurance is as great a need as the basic health care insurance provided by Medicare. The government does not provide this long-term care or insure for it.

6

TAXES AND YOU

UNDERSTAND THE BASICS OF TAXES — AND TAXATION — TODAY AND YESTERDAY

Educated Investors take tax policy seriously. Taxes may help build schools and construct roads, but taxes and tax policy are not always constructive. The Smoot Hawley protectionist tariff in the 1930s helped initiate and prolong the Depression in this country and abroad. And taxes, piled one on top of another, have dampened the creative strength of economies from the beginning of human social interaction.

Understanding the destructive power of taxes is one thing. But Educated Investors also understand some basic tenets of taxation.

The first rule of taxes that Educated Investors understand is that taxes should be proportionate, not progressive — as Adam Smith says in his *Wealth of Nations*. Smith states: "The expense of government to the individuals of a great nation is like the expense of management to the joint tenants of a great estate, who are obliged to contribute in proportion to their respective interests in the estate."

The second rule of taxes is that while modest taxation may be appropriate, too many taxes can be destructive. In Spain during the 15th and 16th centuries, money-making was heavily taxed, and tax policy expressed a contempt for businessmen — in part derived from various religious convictions. The result: Business dried up, and most people wanted to work for the government or achieve nobleman

> **Because wealthy people are often more powerful and sophisticated when it comes to the political process, the graduated income tax in this country became replete with loopholes and began to serve as an instrument of policy.**

status in order to escape taxation.

By contrast, Elizabeth I, Queen of England in the late 16th century, pursued much more lenient tax policies. When she asked for help to defeat the Spanish Armada, her government received far more in contributions from her subjects than she anticipated. Her subjects were grateful for good government and low taxes. Tax policy is obviously critical in many ways.

As of this writing, there is in this country, for the first time in years, serious debate about doing away with the graduated income tax. When it was initially offered, the graduated income tax was a simple and direct plan to charge the wealthiest more money for social services. But because wealthy people are often more powerful and sophisticated when it comes to the political process, the graduated income tax in this country soon became replete with loopholes and began to serve as an instrument of policy. Today, more and more are deciding that it should be done away with altogether in favor of a simpler kind of process. Educated Investors, in favor of simplicity when it comes to money, will probably agree with the basic thrust of this kind of tax reform.

Growth builds the consensus for free enterprise. Stagnation fuels the calls for greater redistribution and socialism. It is growth — not wringing inflation out of the economy by raising taxes to balance the budget — that fires the populist engine of capitalism.

When it comes to investing, Educated Investors will take a long, hard look at a country's tax policies including those that affect individual investments. There is no use in making a profit on an investment if the taxes remove the profit before the investor is paid out.

Additionally, Educated Investors are well aware that since money is produced by credit offered to money center banks by individual central banks, taxes of any kind are mostly a form of wealth redistribution. In our current system of credit-based money, Educated Investors understand that governments need to borrow because it is only through borrowing that government debt is issued. And it is this debt that a central bank purchases and then reoffers to money-center banks. This clever and effective system of credit-based money means the great engine of capitalism runs on debt and will continue to run on debt in the 21st century even if some sort of general gold standard is reintroduced.

In this country, the most recent spate of tax reform produced some relief for those who wish to take capital gains on their investments. There are some other signs that the United States' tax policy is being seriously reexamined on

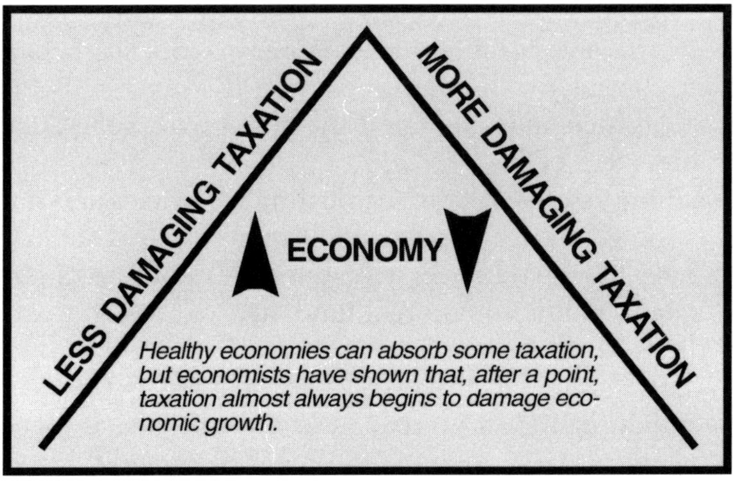

a fundamental level. Hearings have exposed difficulty with certain tax collection policies at the federal level. And a number of plans have been floated to reduce the nation's tax burden or even do away with progressive taxation entirely. Whether these steps turn out to be the first in a new era of reform or are merely cosmetic remains to be seen. Educated Investors will be watching closely.

In the meantime, Educated Investors have internalized one important point: The fewer taxes one pays the more money one has to spend, save and invest. So it is no surprise that people most often seek advice when it comes to taxes. That's the basis of the mad rush to accountants in April each year. Actually the Educated Investor — and his or her advisor — thinks of taxes all year long and particularly when considering retirement.

Understanding taxes means knowing and understanding one's own tax bracket. We are all in the 15% bracket on the first $43,050 of taxable income and the 28% bracket on taxable income between $43,051 and $104,050. As a rule investment income is taxed at one's marginal tax rate, which is the highest rate, usually 28%.

Those living on Social Security benefits alone don't need to worry about taxes after retirement. There are none. Other incomes — pensions, investments, part-time job income — are taxable; in this regard Social Security income can have a distinct impact on the taxable income. Individual filers may pay tax if income is over $25,000 and joint filers $32,000.

Keeping assets intact while dealing with taxes and inflation is the goal after retirement. If money is invested after taxes have been paid once, investment benefits are tax free. Tax-exempt bonds and mutual funds are withdrawn tax free as is the Roth IRA.

When money is invested "tax deferred" this means these dollars can grow untaxed and will be taxed as income when withdrawn. Company retirement plans and traditional IRAs are such investments. When taken out, this money and any growth that it has made are fully taxed. However the retiree may be in a lower tax bracket than when fully employed so will pay less.

Financial gains in the form of stocks, bonds, CDs, annuities and mutual funds are taxed for dividends, interest or capital gains in the same year the profits are made. When they are sold there are more taxes on growth and earnings. Certain tax-free bonds retain income for retirement.

Recent reductions in capital gains taxes work to the advantage of the retired. The capital gains tax rate is 20% for the 28% bracket and 10% for the 15% bracket. These rates are for assets held 12 months or longer. Antiques, collectibles, small business stock and some real estate holdings are not included in this lower rate.

Perhaps the largest tax break for retirees, certainly the most commonly understood, is the one-time, tax-free sale of a primary residence. This is $250,000 for a single person or $500,000 for a married couple filing jointly. Two years prior residence is required. There is no requirement to put the money into another home, so the retiree is free to use the sum to his or her best individual advantage. This is another instance when handling a large sum suggests expert financial advice. A change in lifestyle may be achieved in this instance. Older couples often opt for less space with fewer household responsibilities.

Older individuals who have raised families may anticipate this "lifestyle freedom," and look forward to travel and time for leisure activities. But along with the anticipation of this "golden age" inevitably comes another burden: retirement and health-care planning. While we have already touched on these issues, we will now look at them in more detail.

7 RETIREMENT PLANNING

RETIREMENT PLANNING COMES IN MANY FORMS FOR THE EDUCATED INVESTOR

For the Educated Investor contemplating retirement, planning can come in numerous guises. First is the plan that the Educated Investor may make for himself or herself. Then there is the plan that is done in concert with an investment professional. Finally, there are vehicles that provide a specific planning discipline through a preselected investment vehicle. The vehicles typically include pension plans, profit sharing, employee stock ownership plans (ESOPs) and 401(k) and 403(b) plans.

Lump sum distributions are typical in some company retirement plans, versus monthly distributions. But there are pros and cons to each to consider. In the case of lump sum distributions, additional planning must be made for the lump sum, so as to minimize taxes and maximize the money through rollovers to an IRA or other retirement plan, for example. If a rollover is not done directly to the IRA without the retiree "touching" the money, the IRS can take up to 20% of the money for taxes. If the rollover is planned so that the money does go directly into the IRA, 100% of it will rollover without being taxed at this point.

Educated Investors are aware that annuities and life insurance are other useful approaches to retirement planning. IRAs are also useful if the individual or couple meets the income-specific rules that determine how much can be contributed as a tax deductible contribution.

Home equity is a source of income if the retiree sells and purchases a less expensive home or, instead, rents or leases the home. There are pros and cons to each, including tax and lifestyle ramifications.

Many retirees continue to work at least part time, whether out of choice or necessity. The advantages include socialization, additional income, new challenges, etc. Disadvantages include reduced free time and possible reduction of Social Security benefits if the retiree's earnings pass the program's low threshold restrictions.

It is important that the retirement plan include liquid investments as well as savings and cash reserves for planned, as well as unforeseen, expenses. These might include bank accounts, CDs, money market accounts and funds, and T-bills, as well as tax-deferred annuities.

Corporate bonds are "senior" securities and must be repaid before common and preferred stock, so they are also considered to be liquid investments. Treasury bonds, and tax-free municipal bonds are other types of bonds that might provide liquidity in a retirement plan.

Equity investments have a part in retirement planning. Equity investments include common and preferred stock in individual companies, as well as broader pools of investing such as mutual funds, families of funds, bond mutual funds, government securities funds, municipal bond funds and corporate bond funds; also long-term growth funds, balanced funds and systematic withdrawal programs. Each of these approaches has varying pros and cons as well as varying levels of risk and returns. Mutual funds provide an easy way to invest with a professional and to gain benefits such as "professional selection, diversification, liquidity, choice of objectives, systematic withdrawal plan and ease of record keeping.

While common and preferred stocks are direct stakes in a corporation, there are other indirect ways of investing in equity, such as mutual funds. Mutual funds pool the investment dollars of many and invest the funds under professional management in a number of stocks at a time. This allows the investor to participate in a wider range of stocks than would typically be researchable for one person.

Among the various funds available, there are variations in their approaches. Aggressive growth funds are more growth oriented than municipal bonds, while government securities funds are more income oriented. Specialized growth funds are very growth oriented, and they are also very aggressive; long-term growth funds are also more aggressive. Equity growth funds are less aggressive with balanced funds being even moreso. Corporate bond funds are the most conservative and the most income oriented.

Bond mutual funds include many bonds invested by professional managers for interested individual investors. While individual bonds provide a steady return rate, because this a pool of bonds, the rate of return fluctuates over time. This type of fund provides regular income on a monthly or quarterly basis.

Growth funds pursue a strategy of principal appreciation through capital gains and increasing share value over the long time horizon. Balanced funds provide returns from dividends and capital appreciation; they are comprised of high dividend paying common and preferred stocks, utilities, convertible bonds, and cash equivalents. Systematic withdrawal programs provide the returns of equity plus current cash distributions.

Variable annuities provide the investor with the opportunity to split the investment of their lump sum among a variety of portfolios. The variable annuity provides a range of strategies each with its own advantages; and the annuity builds tax-deferred income. Life insurance products also provide tax-deferred growth and income, as well as federal tax advantages, including tax free loans, withdrawals and death benefits. Investors also try to hedge their investments with tangible assets such as gold, precious gems and rare coins.

Educated Investors will plan for their retirement through patient, disciplined investing. They also will familiarize themselves with various healthcare benefits that are available to them. Medicare and Medicaid planning are part of the retirement plan, as they are available for qualified persons over age 65. Medicaid is designed to care for the needs of poorer individuals and persons who spend down their assets to qualify for the program. Medicare provides benefits to all persons over age 65 for hospitalization and some other healthcare costs; but because it does not cover everything, Educated Investors may wish to purchase supplementary health insurance plans.

Estate planning is the final component to retirement planning. It is the determination of how the assets will be distributed to heirs or other beneficiaries. It is generally comprised of a will, estate and income tax planning, planning for probate costs, living probate, advanced medical directives, etc. More about estate planning next chapter.

If the choice is to take a cash sum, taxes must be withheld by the employer in a lump sum at 20%. Some employer plans allow the money to remain where it is. A 10-year lump sum distribution is available for those born in 1935 or before. However, that is an option for fewer and fewer workers. If a lifetime annuity is an option, a monthly income payment will be paid to the retiree and/or spouse. This is called a joint or survivor option. Benefits cease when both die and usually decrease with the

Corporate bonds are "senior" securities and must be repaid before common and preferred stock, so they are also considered to be liquid investments. Treasury bonds and tax-free municipal bonds are other bonds that might provide liquidity.

death of the retiree. Life insurance for the partner of the retiree can provide income after the retiree's death.

Fortunately, the Federal Government provides a way for retirement money to be free of taxes, at least for a time. It is called an Individual Retirement Account or IRA for short. Most people qualify for IRAs, and penalty-free withdrawals before retirement for certain qualified reasons make the IRA even more appealing. Money should be put directly into an IRA if that is the choice with the check payable to the IRA custodian. Otherwise the 20% tax is due if the money goes through the retiree's account.

The new Roth IRA is an even greater boon for savers. It was created in 1997 by the Taxpayers Relief Act which also liberalized traditional IRAs. The Roth IRA lets everyone who earns income, save. Income restrictions are $110,000 for a single person and $160,00 for those filing jointly. Also money in the Roth IRA accumulates tax-free with no required distribution as in other retirement funds. The money contributed to a Roth IRA is taxed, but its distributions are free to the contributor and/or beneficiaries. The yearly contribution to a Roth IRA can be as much as $2,000.

Early retirement before age 59 is possible with important tax breaks under special circumstances. Called SEPP (substantially equal periodic payments), this withdrawal amount is based on the amount in the IRA and life expectancy of the contributor.

When company stock is part of retirement benefits separating the stock from the rest of the retirement plan may result in a tax advantage especially if the stock has appreciated greatly.

After age 70, those who are retired must begin withdrawing specified amounts from retirement accounts. Roth IRAs are the exception. Again the amount in the account and life expectancy control the withdrawal amount. Penalty for non withdrawal is a 50% tax rate for that not withdrawn.

Everyone must plan for their retirement, but few do.

The average person works hard to earn a living and save a nest egg, but spends less than a single full day actually planning for retirement and distribution of assets.

While most people believe that their retirement income will come primarily from their companies' retirement plans and Social Security, the reality is that these sources will only provide less than half of the income. Personal savings and investments and earnings are the most important sources in reality. Given this reality and the fact that people are living longer today than ever before in the retirement years, retirement planning is critical if one is to live well in the "golden years."

In this chapter we have seen that Educated Investors are proactive when it comes to their retirement. They don't simply expect government or their employer to "do it all." Educated Investors investigate the tools and retirement options that are available to them and then take appropriate action usually including consulting with investment and estate-planning professionals.

8

ESTATE PLANNING

THIS PHASE OF FINANCIAL LIFE REQUIRES SPECIAL DISCIPLINE AND PLANNING

Estate planning is like any other life activity. It either rolls over you, or you take control and make what's occurring work to your advantage.

But setting financial goals and finding ways to achieve those goals requires analysis of where one is and where one wants to go financially.

Some key concepts — at any time of life — are knowing how much we are worth, how much we have to spend and what we can save and invest. Investing to save and saving to invest require systematic initiative often with the help of a professional financial advisor. Becoming familiar with basic concepts such as diversifying investments, allocating resources and minimizing taxes helps the individual achieve control of financial matters for himself. Knowing when to seek professional help in making large decisions such as what to do with large sums requires the individual to become familiar with terms and concepts.

Selecting a strategy to protect assets — especially in one's "golden years" — requires informed decision making. Inflation is a consideration. And taxes — paying the least amount of taxes before and after retirement is the aim of everyone. The goal: Having enough financially to last all of our lives and still having something left over to leave our loved ones.

Let's examine the basics of estate planning.

Wills. In consideration of our loved ones, each of us should have a property will and a health-care will. Maximizing financial organization and resources means minimizing anxiety and dependence on others. Government programs such as Medicare, Social Security, IRAs and tax breaks are there for all of us. It is up to the individual to make the best of each opportunity to better himself in this economy of choices called capitalism.

In addition to the financial power of attorney, Educated Investors will also consider a health care power of attorney — commonly called a Living Will — and also a healthcare directive, which explains their desire in case of medical emergency or long-term medical problems. Let's say your child wants to hold onto you as long as possible. Your don't want to be resuscitated and it's on paper. The hospital will generally honor the child's desire to have you resuscitated because they are not going to be sued for keeping you alive, but they could be sued for letting you go. Make sure you talk to your children so that they are aware of your desires and will not fight your healthcare power of attorney.

Catastrophic illness is the number one crisis facing seniors today. In 1890, the average life expectancy was 37 years old; 1990 life expectancy tables show an average age of 76 years old. We've doubled our life expectancy in the last 100 years. That's great, so long as the quality of life remains good, and the money doesn't run out. But when either of these events occur, those extra years can become a curse as well as a blessing.

The hospital will generally honor the child's desire to have you resuscitated because they are not going to be sued for keeping you alive, but they could be sued for letting you go. Make sure your children are aware of your desires.

Tax planning. Taxes can be devastating to an

estate, but there are ways to minimize them. Couples can take advantage of the unlimited marital deduction to pass assets to the spouse free of estate taxes. However, the heir to the surviving spouse will have to pay taxes due on the combined estate over the $600,000 threshold.

Actually most people think they don't have enough of an estate to worry about planning to avoid estate taxes. At present, estates below $650,000 are free of estate taxes. However one needs to make sure that there will not be a problem by knowing just what value one's estate will have.

There are ways to reduce an expected large tax if the planning is intact. Sums can be given as gifts to children and grandchildren. Mutual funds, securities, educational funds, custodial accounts and life insurance trust funds can be ways of leaving estates to loved ones. The bottom line is that a large estate needs some careful planning by specialists. Other ways to reduce taxes include joint tenancy, trusts, lifetime gifts, estate equalization and charitable deductions.

Avoiding probate. Probate, being a process, is not a tax of itself, but there are taxes and other costs associated with probate — and Educated Investors will want to know about costs, potential taxable events and trouble in advance. A financial durable power of attorney will avoid some of the problems of probate. Educated Investors will realize that it's essential to make sure their financial power of attorney is durable and current.

As with all problems that have a financial component, the key is in anticipation. Educated Investors invariably anticipate — while they can still control events. Educated Investors will consider long-term care insurance because it protects their assets and allows them to have at least some control over how they age and how they will be cared for in case of catastrophic illness.

Why don't more people buy long-term care insurance? Maybe it's too expensive. Or perhaps people believe they're not going to be the one out of two seniors who end up needing long-term care. Perhaps the real reason is that we have yet to see the major wave of people entering long-term care. Just wait until Baby Boomers start aging. Then we'll start to see huge amounts of pressure on the long-term care industry, with prices going through the roof and availability of care going down.

Charities & Trusts. Charities also benefit from generous estate planning through trusts which give income to the retiree while alive and which go to the charity when the retiree dies. One might say that the married have somewhat more time to set an estate right than singles do. A spouse can receive an entire estate no matter how large without estate tax. By 2006, the limit for estate tax will rise to $1 million — an estate of up to $1 million will be tax free. Various kinds of trusts set up with the help of tax attorneys and accountants can shelter spouses and heirs from estate taxes on properties that are higher. Planning is necessary to minimize estate taxes on large estates.

9 INVESTMENT PRINCIPLES

TRAITS OF AN EDUCATED INVESTOR

We've examined some of the planning aspects of Educated Investing. Now let's examine in more detail the basic tenets on which the investment process of Educated Investing is built.

The interaction of our democratic system, its regulatory representatives and the larger marketplace is a fascinating, if sometimes messy, process. While there are always arguments about the political process here and abroad, it cannot be denied that as the world enters the 21st century, the relationships between private markets and public policymakers are broader and stronger than ever.

When it comes to Wall Street, the interaction between public markets and private enterprise is especially evident. The 20th century, with its landmark changes in the U.S. monetary system, including the creation of the income tax and the Federal Reserve — an American version of a European Central Bank — changed the balance of power between bankers and policymakers. Now, as the 20th century ends, we can see the results of these massive changes in terms of an increasingly globalized system that has a good deal of credit available to it through the central banking process. The use of this credit and leverage has been complicated by the introduction of a fundamentally new and powerful tool — the computer.

The computer has not changed the fundamental nature of investing, but it has certainly made it more complex, especially for the world's largest institutional investors and banks.

Derivatives trading is a case in point. Derivatives trading depends on the application of computer power to bundles of securities that are traded — swapped — by international financial institutions in dizzyingly complex transactions. It has been pointed out in such well-respected publications as *The Wall Street Journal* that the amount of leverage — credit granted by central banks to allow member banks to make these transactions — far exceeds total bank assets. A financial crash could trigger an extremely uncomfortable unwinding of these instruments. This kind of discomfort has already been visited on England's former Barings Bank which was closed after tremendous losses in Asian derivatives markets.

Educated Investors will take little for granted when it comes to finance and investing. An Educated Investor will be able to discern significant investment trends and know the signs to watch for as the conflict escalates between proponents of the status quo and those who wish to stretch the boundaries of free markets.

On a more personal level, Educated Investors will take care to insure that their investments are planned and allocated with care. Educated Investors will determine how much risk they can tolerate over time and allocate assets accordingly — with or without the help of a knowledgeable financial advisor.

Educated Investors will familiarize themselves with the basic tenets of Modern Portfolio Theory (we will discuss these later in the book) and use this knowledge to insure that their portfolios are positioned as responsibly as possible.

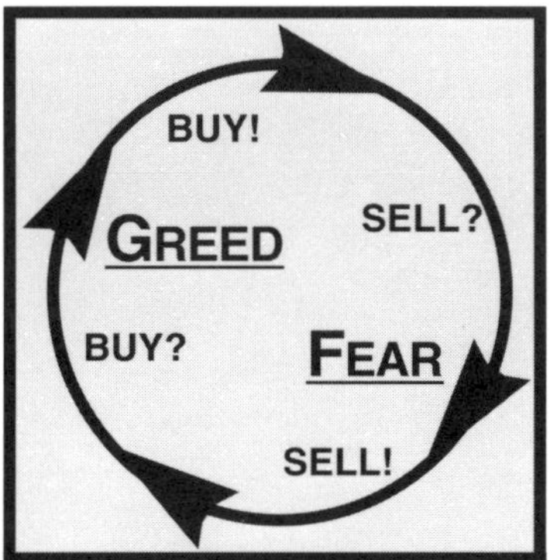

The greed-fear cycle causes uninformed investors to buy at the top and sell at the bottom.

Educated Investors will also try to remove themselves from the **greed-fear** cycle that drives the

> **An Educated Investor will know the signs to watch for as the conflict escalates between proponents of the status quo and those who wish to stretch the boundaries of free markets.**

behavior of most market participants. A knowledge of financial products, the basics of financial history and a determination to build a disciplined portfolio of investments will do much to increase the possibility of investment success.

Educated Investors will never make the mistake of thinking that investing is simple or easy. But in the face of either great success or frightening failure, they will maintain their emotional equilibrium and continue to apply the basic tenets of their hard-won investment education. They will be disciplined despite adversity. They will be skeptical in the face of triumph.

I suppose all this sounds difficult. Please remember, education implies responsibility. And if investing were easy, everyone would be as rich as Warren Buffet!

10

FIRST INVESTMENT PRINCIPLE

NO INVESTMENT WITHOUT FREE MARKETS

The miracle of the "Asian Tigers" (developing Asian countries with booming economies through most of the 1990s) — despite recent stumbles — make it clear that so-called mixed economies can lift people's living standards. What the 20th century has also made clear is that totalitarian regimes that ban the ownership of private property will not last long in head-to-head competition with societies that allow at least a modicum of freedom.

Mixed economies, with sophisticated elites at their head, can often make tremendous strides because the models by which other countries have prospered can be implemented efficiently. Even Russia and China had their "Great Leap[s]" forward. It is when the economy becomes more mature that mixed economies seem to suffer more than freer ones. Japan, with its fairly massive bureaucracy and rigid economic structure was able to mobilize its energetic populace for more than 40 years after the war, but only in the 1990s, after a nearly decade-long recession, did that society's leaders begin to contemplate more fundamental change.

Educated Investors, understanding that freedom allows markets to grow and profits to expand, will always be on the lookout for countries that allow citizens an increased amount of market-based incentives. Incentives, Educated Investors know, are critical to commerce. And chief among these are property rights. Citizens, allowed to partake in the profit generated by their own efforts — and to keep what they earn — expend their energies on projects that may garner them more profits. In this way, individuals benefit and ultimately the larger society does too.

In order to gauge the power and potency of our current marketplace, it is necessary to examine how we arrived here — the roots of our current system.

Most Educated Investors would agree that free markets are based on republican principles of private property, individual freedom and entrepreneurship. This only stands to reason since in a highly socialized state, or in a dictatorship, human rights, intellectual rights and property rights are not respected. And societies that don't honor these rights don't work very well over the long-term. "Mixed" economies — where the State interferes with various rights but does not totally overturn them — tend to work better, but even here there are problems because political interference tends to reduce innovation. Where assurance of profit has been called into question, commerce is impeded.

Rome is a good example of a state that prospered greatly and then fell on hard times as its republican form of government gave way, gradually, to ever more despotic regimes. To begin with, Rome styled itself after the island republics of Greece. The Roman state had little control over the people's daily lives or income. Taxes and tariffs were low or nonexistent, gold was the money of choice and the nation's government and laws were neither onerous nor intrusive. However, Rome eventually became an empire, rather than remain a republic and her vitality was sapped by a succession of despots. As her Treasury

A nation without the support of its people cannot stand. Having become an empire, it was only a matter of time before the Roman Empire was brought low by a combination of military corruption, high taxes and ruined currency.

was drained, taxes went up; tariffs were instituted and a standing — and increasingly mercenary — military force in service of the Emperor imposed the changeable rule of man, not law, on Roman citizens.

Of course, a nation without the support of its people cannot stand. Having become an empire, it was only a matter of time before Rome was brought low by a combination of military corruption, high taxes and ruined currency.

Such has been the experience of nations — and humankind — throughout history. Republics evolve into empires, and empires loot and despoil the citizenry. It was only during the Renaissance, starting around 1350, that Europe began to recover from the Roman tragedy and respect for the rule of law — and the search for knowledge — began to be evident again on a large scale. Great Italian thinkers, nurtured by entrepreneurial city-states, began to explore the entire field of human endeavor, including art, music, even human sexuality.

In England, a despotic king's reign was tamed by the Magna Charta and, later, by the so-called Glorious Revolution that saw increasingly severe restrictions placed on the British Crown. Parliamentary opponents of the king or queen were no longer sent to infamous London Tower to be killed or subjected to rigged judicial proceedings. Habeas corpus was safe. The lot of the average commoner improved, and wealth began to trickle out of the hands of the nobility into a brand-new capitalist class that made money through industry and trade. Eventually, it even became respectable in England to become wealthy through commerce. With the Industrial Revolution in the mid 1800s, the transition from a monarchical agrarian state to a more modern, decentralized political system was well underway.

Economic progress and freedom always seem go hand-in-hand. Throughout history, living standards have been elevated in countries where governments respect property rights and allow citizens to choose their employment and keep most of what they earn. As living standards rise, economies prosper.

In this country, it has often been pointed out, the great exploration of the Midwest was carried out by pioneers who wanted to build on land they owned. They were motivated by ownership. In the East, great mill towns sprang up on rivers from Maine to New York providing power for factories spinning cloth.

There is some sentiment that the entire chapter of Yankee Ingenuity written during the 1800s diminished as 20th century regulations and taxes took their toll. The foundation of U.S. industrial supremacy was laid during the 19th century. While 20th century citizens reaped its rewards, much of what was accomplished in the U.S. occurred because of the freedoms that 18th and 19th century industrialists enjoyed.

Those countries where civil rights are the most respected and where people are left alone to pursue their business the way they see fit are the countries that investors should look for.

Freedom is the greatest enabler of industrial wealth and economic expansion.

11

SECOND INVESTMENT PRINCIPLE

INTERACTIONS BETWEEN GOVERNMENT AND BUSINESS CAUSE BUSINESS CYCLES

Educated Investors understand that successful investing involves more than just familiarity with different kinds of investment vehicles. It involves understanding how economies work, how business cycles occur and what comprises fertile investment ground as investors search to strike a comfortable balance between risk and reward.

Government is a large, powerful and sometimes too-efficient force in the 20th century. In this country, there are many civic and business leaders who have a strong belief in building and maintaining a gently guided economy that will generate an increasingly prosperous society, not only in the United States but — with the help of the United States — around the world.

As with all political and social solutions that leaders expose to their citizenry, there are complications no matter how noble the purpose. When it comes to business and investing, the guidance of top business leaders has specific and recurring economic ramifications having to do with the creation and continuation of business cycles.

In simplest terms, business cycles are a result of monetary policy — usually stimulation. Because monetary policy is increasingly centralized, those charged with guiding economies are also mostly in charge of how much credit is available to banks and businesses. This is where business cycles come in, since if too much money and credit is offered to businesspeople, a boom will result that will eventually lead to a downturn.

Monetary policy is usually conducted by bankers with the help of top businesspeople and policymakers. There are three main ways for central bankers to help stimulate or deflate the economy. One way is for the central bank to buy or sell Treasury IOUs. Another way, which was more popular in the 18th and 19th centuries, is to raise and lower the rates of the so-called discount window, the amount that the central bank charges to its member banks for short-term borrowing. The third way, most popular today, is to move short-term interest rates up or down.

Educated Investors, aware of the ways that central banking policies help stabilize economies, never forget that business cycles are a predictable part of this serious work. Today, booms and busts can be more dramatic than ever. Witness the late 20th century implosion of Asian economies, seemingly overnight. As more money moves around the world more quickly, using ever more complex strategies, economic fluctuations will probably become more, not less, prevalent. Consensus economic analysis tells us that the worldwide stock collapse of 1987 actually began when bankers around the world tightened rates, squeezing the global economy. Markets topped out in 1987, but the downward correction that followed was a thoroughly modern one, enhanced by computers and powerful, if simplistic, program-trading strategies.

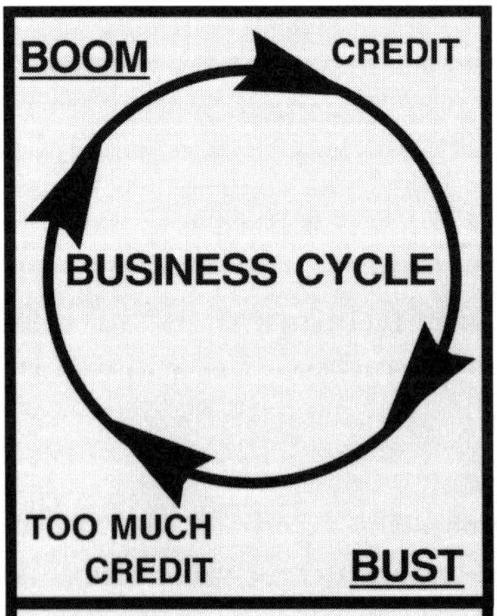

Money and credit stimulate the economy but eventually too much money and credit can cause a recession.

Educated Investors will internalize the trigger points of business cycles, understand that business cycles have been made more

Today, booms and busts can be more dramatic than ever. As more money moves around the world more quickly, economic fluctuations will become more, not less, prevalent.

powerful by computerized trading, and protect themselves and their families through appropriate diversification and asset allocation. More about this in the next chapter.

12

THIRD INVESTMENT PRINCIPLE

ASSET ALLOCATION: THE MOST POWERFUL WEAPON IN AN INVESTOR'S ARSENAL

Educated Investors understand asset-class investing can protect and increase wealth even during the kind of international volatility caused by computer-enhanced business cycles.

Like computers and present-day economic theory, asset-class investing in its most disciplined application is a recently developed science. Its principles, in aggregate, are called Modern Portfolio Theory. Its conclusions, still controversial, are that most investors will be wrong most of the time when they try to actively pick hot stocks and regions of the world to invest in.

While this may be the case, the real world shows us that there are exceptions to every rule. From Warren Buffet to Peter Lynch to William O'Neil, owner of *Investor's Business Daily*, there are numerous examples of individuals who have grown rich picking individual stocks.

Educated Investors may well wish to pick individual stocks in which to invest — with or without the help of a financial advisor. But whether or not Educated Investors are attracted to the wealth that may be generated by individual equities, Educated Investors will not dismiss the precepts of Modern Portfolio Theory out of hand. They are very important. Educated Investors instead seek to be aware of the science of Modern Portfolio Theory and to internalize its concepts.

Modern Portfolio Theory has only developed late in this century. Less than 50 years ago — in March of 1952 — asset-class investing began its development process through what is arguably the most famous insight in the history of modern investing: a paper published in *The Journal of Finance* by a then-unknown 25-year-old graduate student named Harry Markowitz. It is Markowitz who is credited today with forging a new way of looking at how we divide our assets so that we can minimize risk and maximize returns.

Markowitz was guided by one fairly radical assumption. He believed it was possible to scientifically minimize risk and improve returns in a diversified portfolio. Today, some 50 years later, the concepts of Modern Portfolio Theory are gradually becoming more commonly known. Unfortunately, considerable confusion still exists, in part because Modern Portfolio Theory's proponents tend to be academic types who have difficulty communicating what they have observed in terms that are simple enough for the rest of us to understand and to our lives.

The conclusions of Modern Portfolio Theory are valuable, even startling. For one thing, proponents of Modern Portfolio Theory have spent a good deal of time analyzing risk. For most of us, risk is loss of principal. But for Modern Portfolio Theorists, risk is merely the fluctuation of price over time. Various academic think tanks, often funded by institutional money, have spent years seeking securitized instruments (stocks and bonds) that act in similar ways. Those assets that return the most to the investor over time while fluctuating the most widely are the "riskiest" in terms of Modern Portfolio Theory. By gathering together these assets and investing in them as groups — as asset classes — investors using Modern Portfolio Theory attempt to control and anticipate the "risk" — volatility — of their overall portfolio.

As you can see, this is a very disciplined process. Most true asset-class funds are not even available to the general public who must instead make do with various "index funds." While these indexes may be built of like assets, they have not been scientifically designed as true asset-class funds are.

For Modern Portfolio purists, any amount of individual stock picking is too much. These purists argue that only a strict regime of appropriately allocated assets throughout the world can result in controlled profit-making. For those Educated Investors who accept the increasingly incontrovertible proof of Modern Portfolio Theory, but who are aware that the real world is a complex place and that theories do not always translate into reality, Modern Portfolio Theory and asset-class investing can be treated as simply another weapon in an increasingly powerful array of investment armaments.

Like business cycles themselves, asset allocation is an important concept to grasp — but having grasped it, Educated Investors are free to make choices that can enhance their overall profitability without confining their choices within a specific discipline. Educated Investors, aware of Modern Portfolio Theory, will understand that a good deal of profit may be derived from the asset class rather than from an individual equity pick. But, knowing this, Educated Investors may simply choose to allocate a portion of their assets defensively, across asset classes, while still making individual equity selections.

Educated Investors are aware that international diversification yields benefits. But this does not necessarily mean that one should abdicate decision making. Nor do Educated Investors merely restrict themselves to diversification via securities. Educated Investors often diversify their portfolios by holding real estate (a house or an apartment), precious metals such as gold or silver, and well diversified portfolios of equity and fixed-income instruments. These latter investments may be in aggregate (via funds) or individually. Depending on the business cycle, the savvy investor may seek to add or subtract from a given asset class.

13

THREE PRINCIPLES, ONE SOLUTION

COMBINE THE THREE PRINCIPLES OF EDUCATED INVESTING FOR POWERFUL RESULTS

We now understand the three basic rules of the Educated Investor:

—Educated Investors will not commit funds to countries where respect for property rights and free markets is weak.

—Educated Investors are mindful of business cycles as they invest and try to understand the various interactions between governments and markets that spark these cycles.

—Educated Investors understand that Modern Portfolio Theory with its emphases on asset-allocation and long-term commitment to specific strategies is an important investment methodology.

While these are simple rules to understand, they are difficult to follow with consistency and purpose. Understanding general investment rules and making money from them are not necessarily the same thing.

As the investment world grows ever more complex thanks to the use of the computer and the adoption of capitalism including most importantly property rights, in one form or another across most of the world, investors will have to resist the temptation to accept strategies and investment products at face value. Being an Educated Investor will become even harder because of this complexity. The solution to complexity is simplification. That is an investor's ultimate solution. Asset allocation, buy-and-hold strategies are the appropriate mechanism with which to confront the increasingly complex phenomenon of modern investing. Simple tools, but tools that are hard to grasp in the face of so many tempting and contradictory investment messages.

Why is investing becoming increasingly complex? The one main culprit is the obvious one we have already mentioned — the computer.

It is the computer that has given professional investors and academics the tools to analyze investing and formulate the science of Modern Portfolio Theory. It is the computer, too, that is driving investment complexity by allowing professional investors to mix and match different kinds of securities around the world in different market and regions.

Then there is the complicating factor of Wall Street itself. Because Wall Street is so good at inventing new investment strategies, investors will have many more choices to sort through in the future. As additional investment opportunities open up in countries and regions throughout the world, there will be new investments to take advantage of these opportunities.

But the computer is allowing Wall Street not only to gain access to new regions and markets, the computer is making the generation of new investment vehicles intensely competitive.

Investment vehicles already include hedge funds, futures funds, mutual funds, privately managed funds and closed-end funds as well as subsets of each of these funds. Mutual funds, swollen with cash at the end of the 1990s great stock market run, have multiplied until they offer investors literally hundreds of categories from which to choose.

And hedge funds, once developed to offer investors a specific stock market strategy, now offer investors cross-trading strategies that include the use of futures, options and international investing. Closed-end funds may offer investors individual countries in which to invest or increasingly they may offer investors the option of investing in an individual strategy. Thus there are closed-end bond funds as well as closed-end equity funds, and subsets of each of these.

Only by simplifying one's approach to the market, understanding business cycles and the innovation and respect for property that drives wealth, will investors be able to sort through their options with some level of certainty.

Because the business that has built up around investing attracts so many intelligent people who have a good deal to say about various investments' potential and profit, investing often seems complex. Again, the solution adopted by Educated Investors is to take a deep breath and attempt to reduce financial arguments to basics when trying to understand economic debates and broad fiscal and investment issues.

How does simplification help? Take the debate over Social Security, for instance. In this country, investors ought to be free to place the portion of their money that goes to pay for Social Security into the marketplace under their own control. Many have adopted the point of view that such a system would be an appropriate mechanism for wealth production in a capitalist society.

While this is certainly true on its face, Educated Investors will peer deeper. And the deeper issue involved is money creation. Since the Federal Reserve and the Treasury are in charge of putting money into circulation, the real question — a truly simple and powerful one that people need to examine — is how much money is being put into circulation at any one time? If too much money is finding its way into the economy, then there will inevitably be monetary inflation.

Educated Investors therefore understand that the simple act of placing one's cash into the domestic stock market is not, by itself, an affirmation of the magic of the marketplace. Educated Investors, understanding the virtue of simplicity, will also under-

Take the debate over Social Security, for instance. In this country, investors ought to be free to place the portion of their money that goes to pay for Social Security into the marketplace.

stand that no single act of investing, no matter how appealing on its surface, will insure prosperity.

Investing attracts intelligent people. Instruments multiply and become more complex as markets evolve. With so much going on, it is ever more difficult to simplify. But that is what is necessary to be a good investor — an Educated Investor.

In the next portion of this book, we will examine some of the issues that make investing confusing, including regulations, the structure of Wall Street and volatility itself — the up and down movement of markets that often scares investors and makes it difficult for individuals to structure a long-term investment plan they can follow.

14

SECTION SUMMARY

In this section we have examined the goals of an Educated Investor, defined the three basic principles of Educated Investing and examined how these principles can be combined to generate powerful investment results.

We have learned the basic elements of what Educated Investors need to know — that inflation is a monetary phenomenon, that business cycles are the result of too much money and credit and, finally, that the best defense against both inflation and an expansive monetary policy is disciplined asset allocation across investment classes and countries around the world. These countries and regions need to be sympathetic to property rights and have in place market structures to insure that these rights are respected.

We have also learned that the science of asset-allocation has a name: Modern Portfolio Theory. The combination of Modern Portfolio Theory and the computer has given rise to a new class of professional investors whose approach to the markets we will call "New-Style Money Management" — New Money, for short.

Educated Investors — whether professional money managers or informed individuals — build strong portfolios using:

- Free markets.
- Knowledge of what constitutes business cycles.
- Knowledge of Modern Portfolio Theory to generate asset-allocation strategies that react to or anticipate the domestic or international business cycles.

TWO

INVESTMENT ISSUES

15

UNDERSTANDING VOLATILITY

CONTROL EMOTIONS AND BEHAVIOR WHEN CONFRONTED WITH MARKET FLUCTUATIONS

Market volatility may be caused by business cycles, but market volatility and business cycles are not necessarily the same thing. The Educated Investor understands the difference and reconfigures his or her investing approach based on the timing and strength of the business cycle.

It is important to understand both business cycles and market volatility because investing is subject to the twin emotions of fear and greed. Knowledge of how economies succeed or fail can help investors better control their own emotions and behavior when confronted with inevitable market fluctuations.

Before examining volatility, let's reexamine business cycles. In the 20th century especially, business cycles have been generated by government and banking support of the money supply. By offering money and credit, policy makers mix up a heady "punch" that they and the business community are reluctant to have taken away. Unfortunately, the punch bowl must eventually be drained. Money must eventually become worth a little bit less. Credit must eventually become scarcer. Recession sets in. Assets disinflate.

Once people understand these trends, they may see booms and busts around every corner. What we initially comprehend, we immediately anticipate. But the grindingly long business cycle measures itself in decades — understanding its nature and impetus does not mean that we are able to discern its beginning or even its end. The knowledge itself, rather than its market-tim-

> **As the 20th century comes to a close, Educated Investors, having charted the progress of postwar economic expansion throughout the world, are more aware than ever of the breadth and depth of individual business cycles.**

ing aspects, is what empowers Educated Investors.

That business cycles operate within a long timeframe can be seen most plainly (at this writing) in Japan. In this tiny country, middle-class industriousness created a postwar miracle. Powerful regulators, an even more powerful central bank and a highly centralized core of congenial businessmen participated in the country's postwar success but then, over a period of difficult years, this consensual elite had trouble dealing with increased competition worldwide.

At this writing, Germany continues to struggle with relatively high inflation and, more worrisomely, a high rate of unemployment. Additional European countries, especially France, are subject to some economic difficulty. France's national dialogue has even centered recently, on the idea of having the State mandate a shorter work week!

As the 20th century comes to a close, Educated Investors, having charted the progress of postwar economic expansion throughout the world, are more aware than ever of the breadth and depth of individual business cycles. But they are also aware that within such long-term cycles are shorter bursts of frenetic economic activity, tempered by lulls and even inter-cycle downturns, recessions and market busts. This is what we call market volatility — volatility enhanced by the computer. Within the context of investing, the computer is also a magnifying glass, making euphorias move that much faster and making the fall that much harder. Computers are already capable of processing huge amounts of information quickly and coming up with results that allow traders to adjust their positions instantly. Computers are also good at creating new financial instruments.

Computers have burst the artificial barriers set up by financial regulation. They allow big intermediaries, and domestic hedge funds to make quick investment decisions based on the flow of information. Meanwhile, regulations that have grown up over the last 300 years to stabilize the market can work the opposite way in the information age.

It stands to reason that if computers make our financial markets more efficient and if they speed the movement of capital around the world, they can also reinforce dangerous market trends. What may be the first computer driven market crash occurred on October 19, 1987 with the 500 point drop of "Bloody Monday."

It cannot be overemphasized that volatility, like the larger business cycle itself, is a monetary phenomenon. Too much money injected into the economy brings markets to life and moves them up and down quickly. With so much of the world's money supply dependent on credit, it's no wonder that markets go up and down quickly!

Educated Investors, cognizant of what money really is, will use their fundamental understanding of investing to separate market volatility from underlying credit-based booms and busts.

16

UNDERSTANDING WALL STREET

A BRIEF HISTORY OF SECURITIES TRADING AND EXCHANGE FORMATION

In this country, the dominant structural influence on securities trading is the New York Stock Exchange. By any measure, the New York Stock Exchange is one of the nation's and the world's most successful businesses. Shares trading on its floors are routinely in excess of hundreds of millions. The nation's most prominent companies clamor for trading space on its floors. And powerful people from around the world have expressed an interest in touring its halls and seeing capitalism in action as traders and specialists frenetically buy and sell equity in some of the world's most well-capitalized companies.

Listen to the NYSE and you cannot help but be impressed by the statistics that its success has generated. Thanks to the NYSE, as the Exchange is not shy about pointing out, the nation's greatest international companies can count on a vast well of liquidity for their shares along with the credit that liquidity helps guarantee. Truly, the NYSE is a nearly indispensible factor in corporate America's national and international 20th century success.

The NYSE recently announced it might join forces with an overseas exchange to offer investors 24-hour, international trading. With such an increasingly powerful trading presence throughout the world, it is difficult to imagine that the NYSE's dominance was once threatened by a myriad of other New York City exchanges. The most prominent of these Civil-War-period exchanges was an uptown exchange that allowed its members to trade stocks continually. This uptown exchange was gradually wooing brokers and business away from the NYSE which had merged, bought out, or otherwise put out of business many other competitors.

The management of the NYSE was stumped for a while but then, so the story goes, it offered the "Uptown Boys" a deal. If they would close up shop and move to the NYSE, the Uptown Boys would receive certain monopoly rights to stock trading. Thus the arcane yet prominent business of the specialist was born.

Throughout the years, the NYSE has defended its occasionally maligned specialist as someone who insures an orderly market at a physical exchange. The idea is that the specialist, assigned a monopoly trading position in a particular stock, will use his or her own capital to move the stock up and down gradually in "eighths" thus insuring a gradual ascent and descent of stock prices which is most soothing to individual investors. As markets enlarged, the justification for the specialist's role has increasingly became questionable. How can a specialist whose total capital until recently — as demanded by the Exchange — was about $1 million, stabilize a stock whose inflows and outflows could be a hundred or thousand times that? Thus — said critics — the specialists' role was effective mostly when markets were calm (a time when the specialist probably wasn't needed) and ineffective when markets were roiled, the time when the specialist was supposed to play his or her assigned role by purchasing a given stock to "stabilize" it during a panic.

This argument has been partially dampened in recent years by the purchase of family-owned specialist firms by much better capitalized Wall Street firms and even Fortune 500 companies. For critics, such an evolution is encouraging as, these critics say, it is companies and interested institutional investors who should be making markets in stocks anyhow. Those who trade should provide the liquidity.

There is liquidity aplenty during the kind of boomtimes that Wall Street enjoyed in the 1980s and 1990s. In 1993 alone, before 1994's mini downturn, Wall Street passed a historic but little remarked barrier when its top 10 firms broke the trillion dollar mark for public issuance. A handful of perhaps 10 firms issued, incredibly, more than $1 trillion worth of new stock and bond securities, according to Wall Street-based *Investment Dealers' Digest* magazine — some $850 billion in fixed income and $150 billion in equity. This kind of clout is just one small example of how concentrated trading and issuance really is.

The combination of credit issuance via central banks plus the vertical integration of the nation's securities structure is both a positive and a negative, depending on where you stand. A more laissez-faire system would probably be subject to more stresses and strains because the very stratification and control of credit that has emerged in the 20th century allows major money players to smooth out volatility and business cycles. The downside to this system is that it gives a lot of power to few individuals.

Wall Street often seems to be a riddle wrapped in an enigma. Educated Investors will focus on the bigger picture — monetary policy, Modern Portfolio Theory and asset allocation strategies. Market structure and Exchange politics are important to the investment industry itself, but Educated Investors, realizing they cannot change a structure that is the result of hundreds of years of financial evolution, will focus on the allocation and safety of their personal portfolios.

17

UNDERSTANDING REGULATION

WHY EVEN THE BEST REGULATORY INTENTIONS MAY GO ASTRAY

Our regulated markets are the envy of much of the developed and developing world, of that there can be no doubt. The Crash of 1929 and the subsequent regulatory conversation of the 20th century gave the United States a formalized and highly specific regulatory code that still retained considerable flexibility so as not to dampen the entrepreneurial spirit that securities markets were set up to accommodate.

Yet there is always a downside to regulation. It goes out of date, or worse, becomes actively counterproductive. For this reason, Educated Investors will retain a healthy skepticism when it comes to the efficacy of financial regulation. Educated Investors understand that while our intricate financial rulebook may have been conceived with the best of intentions, these rules will not necessarily protect individuals from investment crooks. When it comes to money, Educated Investors follow the dictum: Buyer Beware.

By definition, regulations can only address market problems that have already occurred. They cannot address problems that have not occurred because regulations are drafted to fix perceived difficulties.

Most financial regulation that was passed in the aftermath of the Crash of 1929 concentrated on breaking the power of the banking forces that the common wisdom of that time held responsible for the Crash.

The massive Money Trusts were to be tamed through such regulation as Glass-Steagall which split up banking and securities activities.

Interestingly, at the end of the 20th century, with the announced merger of Citicorp and Salomon Smith Barney, Wall Street has traveled full circle in about 75 years. Now banks and brokerages are getting together again with the tacit acquiescence of Congress, even though Glass-Steagall rules have not been fully repealed.

This brings up an interesting question: What's changed in 75 years so that banks and brokerages can safely function as one unit now when they could not at the beginning of the century?

The answer is probably that nothing has changed. Wall Street was probably not responsible for the Crash of 1929. Many top economists now believe that the Crash of 1929 was due to an enormous expansion and contraction of money and credit by the newly organized central bank of the United States — the Federal Reserve.

As has been exhaustively documented by such Nobel prize winning economists as Milton Friedman, the Federal Reserve caused the great expansion of the 1920s and then the unfortunate Crash of 1929 by expanding money and credit aggressively. It did this in part so that the monetary system that existed before the First World War could again be constructed.

The First World War eroded the English pound's dominance, but after the war, English bankers wanted the pound to become the basis of the world's monetary system. Unfortunately, England had borrowed too much money during the war, thus leaving the American dollar healthier than the English pound.

For this reason, the English central bank asked the American central bank to pump more money into the economy which would tend to weaken the American dollar against the pound. The unexpected consequence of this

If the 1929 Crash and the Great Depression of the 1930s were caused by central banking monetary policy, then what were the regulations of the 1930s supposed to address?

effort was to cause the great boom of the 1920s, since credit expansion always causes booms, and then ultimately the bust of 1929. After this, as Friedman has pointed out, the American Federal Reserve tightened, causing even more problems and pushing the economy into the Great Depression.

If both the 1929 Crash and the Great Depression of the 1930s were caused by central banking monetary policy, then what exactly were the securities regulations of the 1930s supposed to address?

This is a question that has come under scrutiny late in the 20th century. The Securities and Exchange Commission was formed in 1933 to break up what was seen as a clubby group of Wall Street banking firms. The rationale for most of the regulations that the SEC administers — as well as regs administered by the National Association of Securities Dealers and regs that deal with mutual fund and pension plan investing — have to do with insuring that the consumer is treated fairly by those who have financial power.

But if one accepts that the Crash of 1929 and the resultant Depression of the 1930s were initiated by mistaken monetary policy, then one must ask whether securities regulations were the most appropriate response. Why not address the basic issue of monetary policy instead?

Educated Investors may or may not be cognizant of these underlying issues when it comes to regulatory power. But certainly Educated Investors should be aware that the current regulatory situation as it exists in the United States may not entirely address issues that truly need to be addressed.

If there is a question about the efficacy or intent of many U.S. financial regs, there is less question that transparency or "sunshine" is an adjunct to investment health.

Educated Investors look for investments where they are in control of as many pertinent facts as possible. These Educated Investors know that many financial debacles are aggravated by lack of transparency. This lack of information haunted three of the most problematic financial vehicles of the 1980s — limited partnerships, junk bonds, and penny stocks. These investments had one common link; prices were not easily obtained by the average consumer and historical data was, pretty much, unavailable.

The situation is complicated by computer trading, electronic execution mechanisms, and a dizzying variety of new markets and instruments. Expert systems and neural networks, two components of so-called artificial intelligence, further erode traditional investment techniques. Such new technologies make use of computer-generated overviews of investment patterns involving customized universes of securities rather than individual stocks and bonds.

Unfortunately, the opposite is occurring; electronic international nets are being set up by dealers rather than by buyers and sellers.

There is also the problem of single-instrument investing in general. A truly hedged stock fund would be invested in numerous instruments — the idea being that if one market moved one way, another market might move in the opposite direction.

Regulation is changing as the computer breaks down barriers between various financial sectors. The functions of banks and securities firms, separated by Glass-Steagall, have started to come back together in the United States despite controversy, because the electronic market is almost impossible to regulate via industry compartmentalization.

Educated Investors are aware that the 21st century will be especially tumultuous when it comes to financial regulation and may even give rise to an entirely new form of financial regulation that is not dependent on segregating individual instruments and markets. Educated Investors will take care to remember that financial regulations — like military equipment — are too often generated, despite the very best of intentions, to fight the last war. These savvy investors will continue to regard financial fads with skepticism and use, instead, their basic knowledge of human nature and markets to secure the health of their portfolios.

18

UNDERSTANDING WORLD MARKETS

WHY EDUCATED INVESTORS SHOULD CONSIDER INTERNATIONAL INVESTING

Educated Investors are aware that in the late 20th century, international investing aroused criticism.

International investing has come under criticism in part because of the tremendous upwards momentum of domestic securities markets in the 1980s and 1990s. The rate and breadth of the progress of domestic securities markets made international markets less attractive and gave rise to numerous critics of those markets.

It is certainly true that U.S. markets performed wonderfully well throughout most of the 1980s and 1990s. But there are other reasons why international markets have come under attack that have less to do with the vibrancy of U.S. markets and more to do with certain biases that may or may not have their basis in fact.

After all, the media is prone to report on political and economic problems around the world, giving people negative messages. Additionally, international investing does present difficulties in that some countries — especially smaller ones — have corrupt leadership, reporting standards that are lax or nonexistent and money flows from investors and international agencies which are diverted from their intended purposes.

Educated Investors are aware of the biases that the above points tend to impose on domestic investors. But they are also aware that over the past 26 years, the global marketplace has grown explosively while the U.S. marketplace is shrinking proportionately.

Mexican markets crashed in the early 1990s but those same

Mexican markets were top performers in 1997. As of this writing, Asia is having a hard time, but no doubt Asian markets will recover as well.

In 1960, the total value of the world's equity markets was slightly below $500 billion and U.S. equities made up 73.3% of the total value. But by 1990, just 30 years later, the world equity markets had risen to approximately $8.3 trillion in value and the U.S. share had declined to 33%. Although the U.S. market has increased in size in the last 30 years, it has not grown nearly as fast as the equity markets of the rest of the world.

Many foreign government bond markets — including the markets of Japan, the United Kingdom, Switzerland, the Netherlands, Germany and France — have credit quality equal to that of the United States, according to debt ratings by Moody's and Standard & Poor's.

There is no mystery about what builds healthy economies. Low taxes, little regulation combined with high savings rates — so long as these rates are translated into capital for investment — and low, steady interest rates insure that business can plan for the future and invest in a rational way.

A 1993 *Economist* article stated that 96% of U.S. assets were still invested domestically. International investing will be increasingly necessary as the world's equity capitalization expands relative to single region capitalization, even taking into account continued political instability. This is especially true in the United States, where the market cap is expected to undergo massive shrinkage relative to the rest of the world over the next few decades.

U.S markets had a great run in the 1990s, and this run may continue (who knows?) through the early decades of the 21st century and even beyond. But worldwide, the U.S. market cap is shrinking. Educated Investors understand that to diversify and participate in the broadest possible opportunities, they must explore investment options around the world.

Educated Investors recognize emerging markets as a separate and distinct asset class. These emerging countries are experiencing rapid growth and improvements in their political, social and economic conditions.

Emerging market returns are not derived from faster economic growth. Higher returns are a reward for accepting higher risk. Emerging market investing involves substantial risk including political instability, extreme market volatility, lack of liquidity, dramatic currency devaluation, high transaction costs and regulatory risk.

A lack of reliable information is also an issue since many of these countries have inadequate accounting standards and very poor financial disclosure. These risks are much greater than those in developed countries, but they are well known and researched by the market.

Those who can tolerate this kind of volatility are able to participate in the long-term growth of this promising sector of the global economy. In addition to higher expected returns, emerging market stocks give your portfolio another layer of diversification. The correlation of emerging market stocks with U.S. stocks is very low.

Lack of liquidity, tax laws, unscrupulous government and private manipulation of markets, misleading accounting — all of these factors make international investing a tough haul over the long course. Wealth is not accumulated without risk.

COMPARISON OF WORLD EQUITY MARKETS, 1970 & 1996

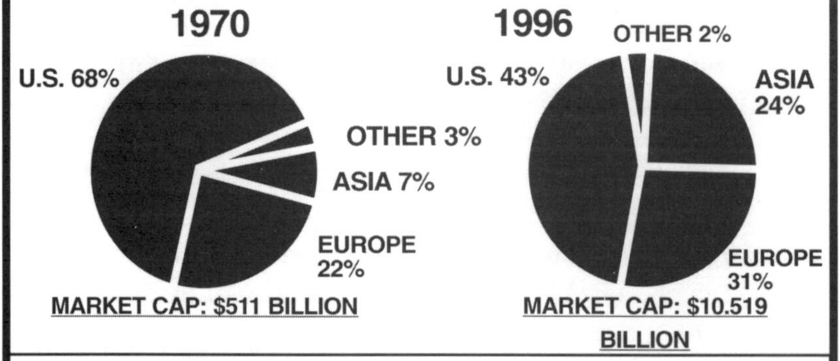

These charts show how United States markets, as part of the world's overall equity capitalization, have diminished in the last 26 years.

Source: Morgan Stanley Capital International

19

FINANCIAL LITERACY

INTERNALIZE INVESTMENT PRINCIPLES — NOT "NOISE" — FOR LASTING SUCCESS

Investing is a big part of life for many of us because taxes, inflation and the ordinary costs of living and raising a family make it difficult to gather and retain a nest egg. Most people spend a good deal of time educating themselves about their jobs, health issues, even major purchases like cars and houses. But the most basic education of all should be an education about money. The Educated Investor — whether by reading this book or by reading or listening to other informed sources — has armed himself or herself with what many would consider basic survival information — if only they knew.

The trouble is that most people don't know where to look to find the investment information they need to know. They may think they've found answers. But often they have not. Those familiar with Modern Portfolio Theory call the phenomenon of investment misinformation — "noise." Noise is information about investing, inflation, business cycles, market timing and other issues that is often contradictory and usually confusing.

If you are reading this book, you are well on your way to becoming an Educated Investor. But you are in the minority. Not only are you becoming an Educated Investor in a short period of time — if you take the information in this book seriously — but you are doing it with considerably less effort than might otherwise be the case. Many Educated Investors take years of effort to arrive at the conclusions we offer herein. They have sorted through the mass of conflicting investment information and painfully arrived at conclusions about monetary issues that often go against the common wisdom available through the major media.

That, unfortunately, is too often the lot of an Educated Investor. As he or she painfully learns the underlying truths of investing, trends become clearer. Signposts loom. Economic direction becomes more obvious.

Educated Investors understand — we have learned — that investing takes place in countries or regions that have constructed some form of a free market complete with the rule of law and property rights. Without such basics, no assurance of profit can be had and thus no investing can take place.

Educated Investors understand what business cycles are and how they work. While business cycles are often mentioned by the media and in financial textbooks, their trigger points, generation and duration are not ordinarily defined. Educated Investors know that inflation comes from money and credit heating up the economy — leading to a boom and finally a rapid disinflation (bust) or slow one (recession).

Educated Investors understand that the antidote to business cycle dislocation is to be found through disciplined asset allocation. Thus Educated Investors are patient investors who will take a long-term buy and hold approach to the market. Nonetheless, they may attempt to reconfigure portfolios based on the timing and strength of the business cycle.

Educated Investors not only understand these three basic principles of market success, they also understand the difference between business cycles and market volatility — the intracycle

Educated Investors not only understand these principles of market success, they also understand the difference between business cycles and market volatility.

ups and downs of the market that do not necessarily signal a fundamental economic event.

They know that while our financial regulations are the orthodoxy of the day, they may not always perform as advertised. They understand that excessive taxes are destructive to economies and countries alike. They are aware of the ramifications of taxes and tax policy on portfolios and investment prospects.

Most importantly, Educated Investors are good listeners. That is, they know how to discern investment noise and listen for what may be important and truthful underneath noise.

Educated Investors, skeptical and informed, are well aware that when it comes to money, truthful messages must be separated with care from the more self-serving elements of noise.

20
SECTION SUMMARY

Educated Investors understand the three basic principles of building a sturdy investment portfolio. Understanding these fundamental points, Educated Investors are in a better position to discern what is market volatility and what economic signs presage more fundamental changes.

Educated Investors are able to separate the mechanisms of Wall Street's trading and investing industry from the underlying fundamentals of monetary policy. These investors are not likely to confuse market structure, nor industry management with changes in economic and market direction. Educated Investors also keep a watchful eye on tax policy, both domestically and overseas. Taxation is not merely a static phenomenon. Changes in the tax code or the way taxes are levied and collected can have a dramatic effect on domestic, regional or international investments and economic prospects.

Educated Investors — whether professional money managers or informed individuals — make a commitment to understanding:

•The difference between business cycles and market volatility.

•How Wall Street works and why structure is less important than monetary policy.

•The ramifications of taxes and the process — and effect — of market and investment regulation.

•The truth about international investing and why too much "noise" can often prejudice otherwise sound investment decisions.

THREE

TOOLS AND STRATEGIES

21
EQUITY

A HISTORY OF STOCKS AND AN EXPLANATION OF MODERN USAGE

Stocks, also known as equity, are a basic investment tool. In simplest terms, stocks allow investors to buy an interest in an enterprise owned and run by others. An investor may purchase private equity in a private corporation or equity in public corporation. It is public corporations we are most concerned with in this book because of the variety of public companies and the creative ways that public equity can be configured, blended and leveraged.

The first stock certificates were apparently issued in France nearly 1,000 years ago to give investors an interest in a mill. France also is responsible for the first formal trading of stocks at what we today call a physical-exchange stock market. At the time, more than 300 years ago, French investors bid to buy and sell stocks in an auction-type environment. In this country, stock markets were initially auction-driven with definite times when investors and brokers met to buy and sell securities.

The first stock market was the New York Stock Exchange and the second stock market was the so-called Curb Exchange which turned into the American Stock Exchange. The Curb Exchange got its name from the brokers who situated themselves on the sidewalk outside the NYSE to trade smaller issues. To this day, the American Stock Exchange makes a business in smaller stocks than the NYSE. When the volume and size of the company gets large enough for an NYSE listing, the company often moves off the Amex.

The last great stock market of the 20th century is the National Association of Securities Dealers Nasdaq electronic marketplace which has now merged with the American Stock Exchange. The Nasdaq market evolved from thousands of small broker-dealers around the country in the 1920s who were brought under one regulatory roof after the Securities and Exchange Commission was set up in the early 1930s. In the late 1960s, the Nasdaq dealers automated so that they could give each other prices electronically on smaller, regional stocks. The only trouble with the Nasdaq market was that dealers could place any price on the electronic quote board that they wanted. This was called a "dealer" market by Nasdaq members since it didn't have a so-called specialist conducting an auction.

With so many markets, stocks and ways of trading, investing in equity can be a fairly complex issue. One way to deal with stock investing is simply to pick top "Blue Chippers." During the 1990s, and to a lesser degree in the 1980s, many investors gained significant returns with this strategy as Baby Boomers began piling retirement funds into the market. Blue Chip proponents argue that this trend will continue throughout at least a portion of the next decade as the nation's biggest stocks are powered continually higher by "Boomer Bulge."

As with any great story, there is another side. Bears (those who are negative about stock market progress) argue — and Educated Investors might sympathize — that great stock markets are inevitably a function of the money supply. According to this point of view, Dow stocks are not the recipient of Baby Boomer largess but convenient vehicles for an overexpansive money supply. These Bears have been wondering out loud if Blue Chips, rather than being a safe haven, are really the riskiest play of all.

Another way of playing blue chip stocks is through the so-called Dogs of the Dow strategy. Based on yield and price, you choose five or ten out-of-favor Dow Index stocks with the idea that these large, successful companies will eventually find their way back into favor. This is a fairly practical strategy, but it is only one of many. There are so many choices that the only way to approach investing, especially equity investing, is with a solid focus and discipline.

Initially, individual investors gathered to buy and sell stock at auction exchanges, but most of these investors were busy men and thus began to designate others to buy and sell securities in their stead. These stand-ins became known as brokers, because they brokered the securities transaction in return for a commission. It was around these brokers that the securities sales industry with its various physical exchanges initially took shape — in France, England and eventually in the United States.

The use of indexed investing was, like derivatives themselves, the outgrowth of a long-term evolution as crisply traced in Peter Bernstein's book, *Capital Ideas*.

Since the 1930s, financial observers, mostly obscure professorial types, have been groping toward mathematically rational forms of investment. There was the Random Walk theory, for instance, postulating that market prices moved by chance and that to try to predict price moves was foolish, if not downright foolhardy. And the theory of the efficient market: An investor might momentarily find a profitable chink in the market's armor, but others would soon follow and the momentary inefficiency would be erased.

Finally, securities theorists like William Sharpe began to pose perhaps the largest question of all: Can anyone truly beat the market? In the 1970s there was an explosion of quantitative strategies, mathematical methods of investing through indexes. Mainframe computers churned out lists of stocks to be bought and sold.

Today, the basic tenets of Modern Portfolio are increasingly becoming part of sophisticated investors' arsenal. However, these concepts, far from shrinking investors' available options, have merely reconfigured them. With the increasing acceptance of Modern Portfolio Theory approaches, investors purchasing stock must decide between passive, active or technical analysis to determine what equities they wish to hold.

Active stockpicking of individual equities is perhaps the most common kind of strategy for individual investors. This strategy is also the most easily understood by the individual investor since an individual stock comes with a "story" — a reason why it ought to be purchased. Sometimes the story has to do with a hot product the company is supposedly marketing or maybe the special situation of the company within its industry.

Unfortunately, many times investors who pick stocks based on stories about them are misinformed, ill-informed or simply too late since markets are efficient and most available information is factored into them by professional institutional and retail investors long before the individual investor gets ahold of it.

Another kind of investing is often referred to as **Passive.** This is a more recent kind of investing based on Modern Portfolio Theory which calls for buying and holding larger groups of stocks without attempting to pick them individually. The reason to buy large groups of stocks that represent an "index" or asset-class — equities that tend to throw off similar returns over time — is because Modern Portfolio Theory holds that individual investing does not add value to a portfolio and that the best an investor can do over time is track the market. This finding, which has gained support over the last few decades, is obviously a difficult one within the industry with many supporters of active stock selection pointing to individuals like George Soros, Warren Buffet and Peter Lynch to buttress the contention that some active stock pickers can do

Unfortunately, many times investors who pick stocks based on stories about them are misinformed, ill-informed or simply too late since markets are efficient and most available information is factored into them.

well despite the findings of Modern Portfolio Theory.

Finally, there are those who subscribe to technical analysis in various forms. **Technical analysis** can be applied to more than just stocks and has either broad or narrow application. Some technical analysts who have gained fame use technical overlays that purport to chart the historical movement of a given security or asset class over hundreds or even thousands of years. Then there are those analysts who apply narrow-gauge pattern research to equity movement, analyzing individual equities to isolate patterns that repeat in predictable fashion. The idea is to spot an emerging pattern and invest in that stock or asset class before the trend is obvious to others.

Many investors, professional or not, combine parts of all the above strategies to create their own proprietary formulas. But despite the complexity of some of these formulas, the basics of investing — one that applies to almost any kind of securities purchase — is that one needs to adopt a disciplined, even rigorous approach that emphasizes the longer term and includes reallocation rather than the quick buying and selling of individual assets.

While some professional traders as well as "day-traders" trade in and out of the market dozens if not hundreds of time in a day, eking out trading profits using a variety of electronic trading tools, this is not the preferred solution for most investors concerned with keeping up with inflation and securing at least the possibility of a solvent retirement.

22 FIXED INCOME

TYPES OF BONDS AND MODERN USAGE

Bonds are basically IOUs issued by one party and purchased by another. Bonds differ from stocks because the purchase of stock gives an investor a stake in the enterprise from which the stock has been issued. Bonds, however, are a claim on assets of the company or an institution, not an ownership participation.

Bonds are also referred to as debt just as stocks are also referred to as equity. When investors purchase a bond, they are allowing a company or institution to make use of their money for a specific period of time before receiving back the principal. The date at which the principal is returned is called the maturity. Since there is no profit to investors for the risk in lending money to a company or institution if they merely receive back their principal, investors who lend funds are compensated through the regular payment of interest, often called a coupon.

Bonds fluctuate in price, depending on the progress of the issuing company or institution, as well as the larger interest-rate environment. Traded in the secondary market, bonds are bought for a price either higher or lower than the "par" price at which they were initially issued. If a company is doing especially well, its bonds may go up in value since investors will perceive that the risk of not receiving back the principal on that company's bonds is less than it was when the bonds were initially issued. The fluctuation of bond prices, when combined with the value of the bond's rate of return is called yield. The yield fluctuates inversely to the price. When a bond trades higher, the yield falls and vice versa. Bonds with high yields — often called "junk" — tend to be riskier than bonds with low yields.

The most common kinds of bonds purchased by investors are not actually company bonds at all. Instead, they are U.S. bonds of various maturities backed by the faith and credit of the U.S government. Longer-term bonds are called Treasurys. Short-term instruments of less than a year are usually referred to as Money Market funds. U.S. Treasurys are commonly thought of as "safe" because the backing of the U.S. government is said to virtually guarantee the investor's principal. (Critics of U.S. fiscal policy point out that U.S. Treasurys may not be so safe as they seem. The national debt of the United States is close to $15 trillion when unfunded liabilities like Social Security are included.)

Another kind of bond backed by the government is the municipal bond. This bond is called municipal because it is not issued by the Federal government but by state and local governments. There are several different kinds of municipal bonds but the attraction, over-all, of these bonds is that they are often backed by the full and faith and credit of the issuing authority and that they are tax advantaged to varying degrees. While municipal bonds may seem to be great buys, the trouble with them is that the state and local

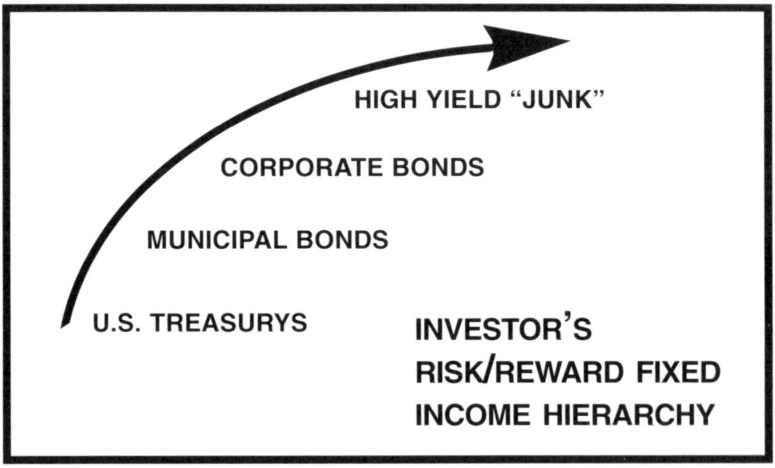

> **The ease with which securities can be created with computers has given rise to a fairly new phenomenon in which equity and debt instruments shade into one another.**

governments often "call" them when the economy is doing well and the bonds' prices are rising. When a bond "tranche" is called, investors receive the full face value of their bonds but, having received this face value, their bonds are thus redeemed, sold back to the issuing authority. No more interest is due. The lending contract is void.

This happens because the state or local authority knows it can issue new bonds with lower rates, thus saving money. For investors, such a "call" may seem unfair since the investor is not being adequately rewarded for the risk that was initially undertaken. Calls take place regularly in the muni market but not in the Federal Treasurys market. Corporations may be reluctant to call bonds because of the pressure that investors can bring to bear and the resultant bad publicity.

The tax-advantaged status offered by municipal bonds may also be scrutinized by Educated Investors. A hardheaded analysis of the total return on tax free municipal bonds doesn't seem to justify the lack of taxes. Municipal bonds have high trading costs. There are large bid/ask spreads and significant market impact costs in the municipal marketplace.

The fragmentation of securities and the ease with which different kinds of securities can be created with computer power have given rise to a fairly new phenomenon in which equity and debt instruments increasingly shade into one another.

One such example of this is the so-called junk bond sector that received so much attention in the 1980s when Michael Milken and Drexel Burnham Lambert began to refinance the debt of promising companies with past credit problems. By offering the bonds of these companies at low prices and with high dividends, Milken and Drexel figured out how to tap funding from first the institutional market and the larger retail market. While the "junk" market, which Milken always liked to refer to as "high yield," doesn't receive so much attention these days, it continues to thrive with major Wall Street players as well as institutions and individual investors willing to purchase the debt of companies that have seen dark days but are on the mend.

Investors can buy individual bonds from companies or they can buy bond funds. Bond funds have become extremely popular in the 1990s, growing as the popularity of mutual funds (public funds in which investors can buy shares) themselves have grown. Like stock funds, bond funds ride on the back of interest rates. The low interest-rate environment of the 1990s worked to the advantage of bond funds. With the exception of 1994, when the Federal Reserve hiked interest rates six times, causing havoc in the bond market and actually helping to bankrupt California's Orange County, bond funds and bonds in general were a forgiving investment throughout the mid 1990s.

In both the 1980s and the 1990s, bond funds received a good deal of cash. In the 1980s alone, one fund went from $800 million to $8 billion under management in just a few years.

The downside to bond funds is that while low interest rates tend to allow these funds to attract new money based on past returns, the blended rate of return these funds can offer must invariably decrease as rates continue to trend downward. Thus, bond funds tend to resort to options-writing strategies and other methods to force their rates of return higher. Such artificial stimulants work well until a sudden market event moves stocks down and bond investors are startled to find that their bond funds are more closely tied to stock prices than they had been led to believe. This happened in 1987, and again in 1994. It will continue to happen.

Bonds are purchased by investors who want regular returns. In a low interest rate environment, bonds can seem to be a fairly safe purchase. But Educated Investors know that bond funds can also be volatile, that the tax advantage and assurance offered by municipal bonds may be illusory and that even the safest of all bonds, the "plain-vanilla" Treasury, has its critics. Bond funds themselves, can be volatile and the most popular recent instrument on the market, junk bonds, have as much in common with equity, in terms of performance and volatility, as they do with debt.

There is no free lunch. There is no totally safe investment. The domestic interest rate environment was low throughout the 1990s and inflation was thought to be low as well. Thus bonds appeared, for the most part to be a good investment for those who did not want to participate in the stock market. Of course throughout most of the 1990s, the stock market's gains were tremendous and thus bonds, when seen from a total return basis, didn't prove to be such good investments after all.

For bond bulls, the seeming certainty of the coupon's arrival as well as the apparent surety that one's principal has not been placed at risk, are the overwhelming reasons to invest in fixed income. What Educated Investors know is that the purchase of bonds or bond funds may actually be more of a barometer of individuals' psyche and innate risk tolerance than an economic necessity.

23

TANGIBLE ASSETS

HISTORY OF TANGIBLE ASSETS AND EXPLANATION OF MODERN USAGE

Tangible assets consist of commodities, precious metals and real estate. They are the final large piece in the investment puzzle for the individual investor. Tangible assets are purchased by investors for different reasons than securities and perform different functions within a portfolio.

If one accepts the argument that inflation is basically a monetary phenomenon, then one must also grant that the money stock, issued from central banks via actual paper money as well as credit, is bound to go up over time.

In the case of central banks, it is often said that these good, gray bureaucrats, no matter how well meaning, simply cannot determine how much money and credit is too much. And, because of the political pressure to increase the money stock, inevitably too much money will be issued into the economy, sooner or later causing a boom and then, perhaps, a bust.

It is for this reason, that Educated Investors like to hold instruments in their portfolios other than securitized assets like stocks and bonds. If one accepts the argument that the value of money must erode in the current monetary setup, then one will leaven his or her portfolio with assets that are more erosion proof. This is the argument, in simplest terms, for rounding out one's portfolio with a dose of tangible assets.

Someone who purchases a stock or bond, for instance, may buy a little bit of a physical plant but chances are he or she is making the purchase to acquire the intellectual capital of the company, its prospects, the skill of its management, the positioning of its products.

Tangible assets are purchased primarily for their intrinsic worth. People do not purchase a house or a bushel of wheat to take advantage of a management style. People buy hard assets to protect themselves from inflation and because they are uncomfortable with ownership of only securitized assets.

Of course anything can be securitized and the computer is making the securitization of hard assets more feasible than ever. There are, for instance, Real Estate Investment Trusts (Reits) composed of various construction projects that trade on stock exchanges like closed-end funds. Another way of securitizing real estate popular in the 1980s was through limited partnerships. In this form of securitization, general partners created a money raising venture and then offered it to the general public. As the general public eventually found out, many of these deals were flawed, offered more for the fees — that the sellers could put in their pockets — than for any eventual underlying value.

The nation's commodity exchanges including the big two Chicago-based marts, the Chicago Mercantile Exchange (Merc) and the Chicago Board of Trade (CBOT) have been adept in the 1980s and 1990s at offering investors bundled products composed of underlying commodities like grain and metals.

What certainly remains incontrovertible, however, is that the market for tangible assets is at heart a market set up for a function — hedging — whereas securities markets dealing in the buying and selling of companies and their intellectual property is at heart a speculative market. This can be seen when one traces the evolution of commodities markets back to their source in China where they were set up over 1,000 years ago to trade rice and grain. Farmers — then as now — had a reason to want to trade commodities because prices fluctuate. By locking in a price, farmers could be assured that they would receive a certain amount of money for their crop. Today, commodities trading is international business with the same kind of worldwide trading mechanisms, institutional traders and trillion-dollar markets as securities trading.

While there have been, and continue to be, energetic attempts to make commodities markets more available to the general investing public, commodities markets were set up and will remain markets with a specific industrial purpose. The industrial purpose of these marketplaces can be seen clearly in the amount of leverage that is built into them. The leverage allows the farmer or raw materials producer to lock in prices with a relatively small amount of cash. But for small investors, that useful leverage is actually an impediment since small moves in the price of commodities can result in a "margin" call that, if not honored, wipes out the investor's stake.

The futures industry has fought to bring its products more into the mainstream of investments through something called managed futures. However, the fees charged by managed futures are quite high. Until managed futures fees come down as real competition blows through the industry, the offerings by commodity trading advisors will remain flawed. As the industry matures, there may start to be a greater variety of investment strategies and fee structures offered. Trend followers even now have a lot of different options. They can override their computerized strategies, follow discretionary trend systems, or be intuitive.

For small investors on the commodity exchanges, the farmer's useful leverage is actually an impediment since small moves in the price of commodities can result in a "margin" call that can wipe out the investor's stake.

The dilemma of the futures industry is that having pioneered large-scale derivatives trading, the industry has not yet succeeded in making those same derivatives available in any meaningful way to the smaller investor.

We have now examined Reits and commodities. The third popular tangible asset class is precious metals.

While there are many precious metals, the ones most investors purchase are silver and gold because of their history and relative availability. Precious metals are not simply precious because someone decided one day that they would be. Precious metals, especially gold, received this status through a process of marketplace competition.

Throughout history, people traded with a number of different kinds of entities — salt, shells, gems as well as precious metals. Ultimately, gold became the leading repository of value for most of the ancient world. It was light, beautiful, malleable and serviceable. Silver, with many of the same properties, was a close runner-up. Once gold was established as the money metal of choice, it was often stored in warehouses. And as these warehouses became more commonplace, they began issuing receipts to businessmen — receipts that could be used in place of gold. These receipts are what we know today as checks.

The monetary system, as man first constructed it, was relatively simple. Businesspeople, perhaps, paid owners of warehouses for the convenience of storing gold. Later on, warehouse owners began to lend gold overnight and thus could diminish what they charged for storing gold and even pay businessmen something per ounce as an incentive to store gold with them.

The final evolution of the warehouse system saw the warehouse owner beginning to lend out large quantities of gold from his stores — stores he didn't own. Today, this practice is known as fractional banking and is the accepted form of banking around the world.

Given the complexity of the monetary system and its propensity to inflate away the value of paper money, the investor would do well to have some sort of tangible asset in his portfolio. As we have seen, the purchase of commodities such as grain or wheat is probably beyond the grasp of the average investor due to the leverage built into the trading of these products.

The simplest way for an investor to add tangible value to his or her portfolio is to hold real estate — such as a house or an apartment. Another way of holding tangible assets is through the purchase of jewelry. In developing countries the gold bands, bracelets and earings that women wear often constitute the bulk of the family's disposable wealth. Finally, one can simply buy gold, either coins or bars. The grimmest purchasers of gold actually buy gold coins and store them in some readily accessible facility, anticipating a day when paper money and credit will be less in demand than this age-old medium of commerce.

24

MONEY STRATEGIES

EMERGING INVESTMENT STRATEGIES COMBINE MARKETS AND INSTRUMENTS IN INNOVATIVE WAYS

Initially, investing was conducted through paper contracts (certificates) traded through the mail or on the floor of a physical exchange. But, just as they have changed so many other things, computers are rapidly realigning how investing happens and even what an investment is.

Without the computer, it was difficult to trade more than individual, discrete instruments. But the advent of the computer allows professional traders and investors to bundle securities electronically, to mix them up, match them differently and hedge them in unusual ways.

There is the story of a top trader who recently set up his own shop to bundle securities in unusual and complex ways, using arcane, mathematical formulae. By making the bundles of securities exceedingly complex, this trader managed to disguise how much they were really worth. He made his profits simply by understanding the mathematical relationships better than the Wall Street "rocket scientists" with whom he was trading.

One must be very careful in applying "new" to anything that has to do with financial instruments. However, it is certain that the application of computer power to investing has added complexity to investing and is gradually, but radically, changing the types of instruments that are being traded.

It has even been hypothesized that computers are starting to create two discreet markets in the world. First is the broadly based market of historical instruments like stocks and bonds. Second, at an institutional level, are bundled securities, replete with hedges and derivative bets traded by large financial entities with billions at stake.

Faced with this evolution in securities trading, it is useful to try to define the different kinds of strategies that are being employed. Using this formula, one can discern various historical and strategic layers of management. Since this sort of evolution is relatively new, there is no nomenclature to define it. For lack of better terminology, we will call the various kinds of evolving fund strategies Big Money, New Money (we've already discussed this) and Hot Money.

Big Money: The first and most accessible layer of money management is that provided by mutual funds. A mutual fund is usually managed by a financial firm to invest in securities on behalf of investors who purchase shares in the fund. These shares are invested in aggregate by the managers of the fund who then pay out dividends depending on the fund's performance. If the fund does poorly, the participant (investor) in the fund may receive less money than he or she placed in the fund should that investor wish to redeem shares. On the other hand, if the fund does well, the investor will see the value of his or her shares climb.

Mutual funds are supposed to invest in strategies, markets and instruments that are specified in the fund's charter. On the surface, this makes funds a good investment tool for individual investors who may want to diversify their assets across several different kinds of markets and strategies. What investors have learned to their dismay is that sometimes funds do not invest in what they have identified as their target product or strategy. This is called mutual fund "drift" and it is a chief reason why investors should try to keep track of their funds' investment mix as much as possible. An investor, for instance, who believes that his fund is investing in blue chip stocks when the fund is actually investing in smaller stocks to try to generate increased performance, may have entirely the wrong idea about how his assets are really dispersed or diversified.

There are several variants of mutual funds. Most mutual

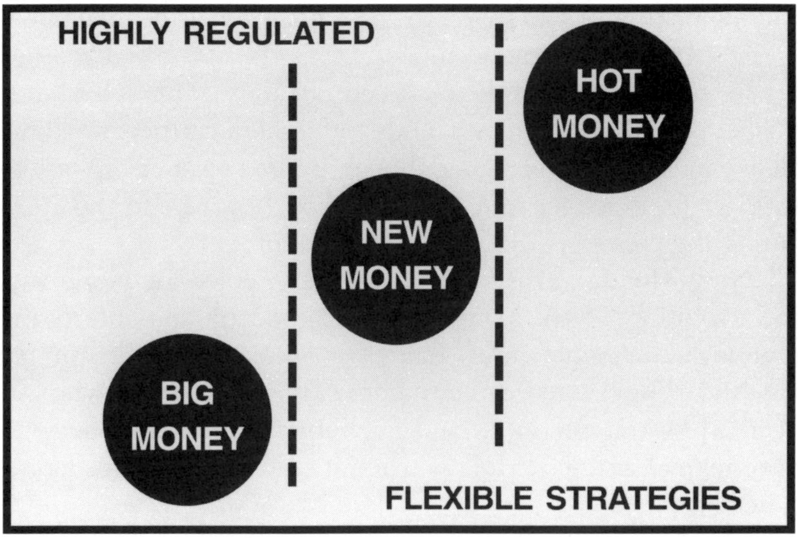

funds are open-ended, which means that fund managers will continue to accept investors' cash even if the fund has been in existence for a period of years. As mutual funds' popularity have increased over the years, some fund managers have taken to closing their funds to new investors. This is usually done when the fund manager or company management feels that the fund has grown unwieldy and difficult to invest.

Another variant of the mutual fund is the closed-end fund that trades on various physical stock exchanges. These funds are actually launched publicly and the difference between a closed-end fund and a plain-vanilla mutual fund is that shares are not valued at the underlying price of the fund's investments. Instead, the shares are valued at a market price that may be different — less or more — than the value of the underlying securities in which the fund is invested. This makes closed-end funds attractive to some investors, especially professional investors, who track the value of closed-end funds' underlying shares with the intent to purchase shares when their publicly traded value is less than the value of the aggregate underlying securities.

In this country, public managed money got its start in Boston, Massachusetts, where funds like Fidelity organized purchasing pools and sold shares in these pools to the general public — thus the name "mutual" funds.

In the latter half of the 20th century, mutual funds and their smaller brethren, closed-end funds and limited partnerships, have all expanded in popularity — though limited partnerships at this writing are no longer so well regarded as they were in the 1980s during the prolonged S&L real-estate runup.

New Money: This kind of investing, emerging along with the evolution of the computer, is significant and interesting. Unlike public mutual funds, many New Money funds are run privately by Registered Investment Advisers (RIAs) who are licensed by the Securities and Exchange Commission but who have many less rules to follow when it comes to how this money is managed.

RIAs run private funds that are oftentimes bundled by Wall Street firms to form so-called "wrap programs." These programs offer investors a choice of different money managers depending on the amount of risk the investor is willing to undertake and the strategy the investor seeks.

Brokers who offer Wall Street wrap programs charge quarterly or annual fees ("wraps") and in return supposedly give the investor access to the busy money manager of his choice.

Wraps can also be built from mutual funds. And many RIAs start out as private money runners and then graduate to running mutual funds as well. In such cases, these money pros will often manage private and pension plan money in much the same way as they do their other pools of capital-following Employee Retirement Income Security Act (ERISA) rules and single-asset investment strategies for both portions.

New Money is larger than any single strategy. In fact, in the future, investors may well take into account strategy and style as well as asset-class diversification.

The investor, for instance, may not wish to take sides in the controversy between efficient market money pros who invest through indexes and those money pros who continue to make a living successfully picking out individual stocks. The investor may diversify among diversified funds, with arbitrage funds — funds that perform intermarket hedging. As the computer breaks down securities segmentation, more and more choices, strategies and markets will be available to the individual investor.

New-Money managers can perform arbitrages between different asset classes in different countries, can utilize market-timing strategies generated by artificial intelligence programs, and can develop sophisticated hedging and short-selling tactics around the world.

As regulatory impediments lessen and information becomes increasingly available, the nomenclature becomes less important even as the profit — and risk — increases. To complicate the picture, a whole new wave of trading software is about to slosh over the global scene that has to do with new kinds of software just now starting to be used by traders: Artificial intelligence (AI). Once considered an esoteric and highly limited way of analyzing vast amounts of complex data, AI — or the use of advanced software that is capable of being "trained" to "recognize" specific developments (such as price patterns and trading volume changes) — is now being viewed as an increasingly viable tool (despite a variety of setbacks and disappointments) in the investment arsenal.

In the latter half of the 20th century, mutual funds and their smaller brethren, closed-end funds and limited partnerships have all expanded in popularity, though limited partnerships are no longer so well regarded as they once were.

As more and more corporations and day traders use this kind of technology, the market's velocity, its interday trading movements, increase dramatically. It would be nice to wish away the effects of modern technology in the world's marketplaces, but the kinds of macromarket trading that computers allow will increase, not decrease, in the coming years.

But true deflation-reflation hedging lies, at least to some degree, outside the securities markets — in Hot Money.

Hot Money: For purposes of this book, Hot Money is money invested in commodities or some other tangible but securitized asset. The problem with purchasing tangible assets is that it's difficult to purchase enough different classes to be properly diversified. It may be better to purchase at least some assets through futures funds. Additionally, because of the way commodities markets are structured, Hot Money is usually leveraged to some degree. And this is a reason it is often called "hot." Such leverage can lead to quick, large losses.

Hot Money remains hostage to the futures industry that is still largely built around physical pit trading, domestically at least. This tends to generate an inbred trading environment in which professional insiders gain an edge over everyone else, including customers. Until the commodities industry, including regulators, comes to terms with its electronic future, the industry's potential will remain relatively untapped.

25

IPOS & SPECIAL SITUATIONS

UNDERSTANDING INITIAL PUBLIC OFFERINGS, SMALL STOCKS AND DERIVATIVES

We have examined basic investment tools Educated Investors use to build their portfolios. In this chapter we will examine additional tools, such as small stocks, initial public offerings and financial derivatives including options and stock index futures.

Educated Investors may or may not wish to use these tools. Certainly they are not necessary when building a long-term, defensive portfolio. However, Educated Investors want to understand as much as they can about all markets and instruments. A broad understanding builds a broad frame of reference which is a valuable commodity itself.

Small stocks: Small stocks are among the most misunderstood investments available in the marketplace because the amount of money it takes to get involved in small stocks is not so large as the amount of money it takes to become a factor in the movement of large stocks. This means that unscrupulous securities salesmen who lack cash can still take advantage of investors by dangling tantalizing low-end stock opportunities before clients — opportunities that can turn out to be outright frauds.

Having said this, it is necessary to point out that small stocks can turn into big stocks and that a purchase of the right stock at the right moment can result in the kind of gain that is not feasible with big stocks. After all, even Microsoft was a small stock once.

Smaller stocks can be found on such exchanges as the Nasdaq electronic exchange and, to a lesser degree, on the American Stock Exchange.

IPOs: One way to take advantage of promising situations is to buy an initial public offering or IPO. IPOs are brought to market by various securities firms as part of a selling syndicate. IPOs are often sought after by those with an interest in getting on board at the beginning of a company's exposure to public securities markets. In the long-term, many IPOs do well, but in the short term, because of the difficulty in establishing value, IPOs tend to fluctuate and many companies which are brought to market at prices that are too high for the stock to sustain, move down for a time. Like any other kind of investing, investing in IPOs is a discipline that demands patience and the ability to discern value.

Buying an IPO is a kind of bet — the investor is making a statement of faith. For investors who enjoy even franker bets, the securities industry offers even franker bets through the use of such instruments as stock options and other so-called derivatives.

Derivatives — options, stock index futures: There are two kinds of exchange-based stock derivative products currently operating in the United States: options and futures. Options allow investors the right to buy or sell an asset or instrument at a given "strike price." Futures confer an obligation for the investor to buy or sell at a certain time and price. Call options allow the investor to buy at certain times and price; put options allow the investor the same right to sell. Futures are dealt in contracts to buy or sell a certain amount of a commodity or financial instru-

An IPO marks the beginning of a company's exposure to public securities markets. In the long-term, many IPOs do well, but in the short term IPOs can fluctuate dramatically.

ment at a specific price, to be delivered at a specific time in the future. In the 1990s, derivatives have traveled off-exchange to be applied by Wall Street in ever-more customized formats as hedges for individual, institutional transactions.

Options involve special risks and complexities and are not suitable for all investors. A current Options Disclosure Document is available from us, the Zhangs, by written request to the Zhangs at 5136 Lovers Lane, Suite 200, Kalamazoo, Michigan 49002.

Variable annuity contracts and their underlying subaccounts are subject to market risk which causes their value to fluctuate.

The Chicago Board Option Exchange, once a subsidiary of the Chicago Board of Trade (CBOT), pioneered options trading in the early 1970s by standardizing contracts and by fixing expiration months and the times of strike prices. Today, options are traded in several ways on U.S exchanges. The Pacific Stock Exchange and the CBOE use market makers to insure liquidity; the Philadelphia Stock Exchange, the American, and New York use specialists.

Exchange-traded options flourished in the late 1970s and into the 1980s despite the competition from financial futures. But as the 1980s evolved, the preference of the industry's powerful institutional investors tipped toward financial futures, especially stock index futures, because of the ability to trade an index instead of an individual instrument.

The first organized futures exchange, the CBOT, was formed in 1848. Today, 16 domestic exchanges are authorized to trade futures contracts; only about 1% of the futures contracts are now settled via delivery of the underlying product. Trading, standardized as to month of expiration, quantity, and quality, takes place in the "pit" between floor brokers, representing customers' orders and locals, the floor traders trading for themselves.

Futures contracts on financial instruments such as interest rates and bonds were developed on various commodities exchanges in the early 1970s. Stock index futures create the obligation to receive or deliver the equivalent, in cash, of a certain group, or portfolio, of stocks.

Stock index futures are based on the weighted average of stocks represented in the index; they were almost an immediate hit with institutional investors, especially those who were broadly invested in the Standard & Poor's 500. Since the performance of the S&P 500 was the gauge by which institutional performance was based, most institutions using quantitative trading techniques were interested in tracking the index in as many markets as possible.

The Merc S&P 500 Index soon became the most popular stock index futures contract, accounting for some 80% of the volume. Such trading was a natural outgrowth of the tendency for the market to be dominated by bigger and bigger investors — pension plans and money managers. Between 1955 and 1980, the NYSE found the holding of its listed stock by selected institutions grew tremendously, to nearly half — and more than half of all trading done on the NYSE was on behalf of institutions.

26

ANNUITIES, INSURANCE, PLANNING

LOOKING BEYOND THE MARKET FOR RETIREMENT TOOLS

The main thrust of this book is to explain what money is, how it is invested and how Educated Investors use that knowledge to come up with better ways to save it and make it grow.

Within this context, we have examined a broad range of issues from market structure to various securities instruments. An adjunct to these investment instruments are annuities and insurance.

Regulation tends to make financial instruments dissimilar. Computers tend to make financial instruments similar. It is interesting to note, as the 21st century begins, that it is the similarity between instruments that is surging to the fore. Banks increasingly offer securities. Wall Street is ever-more heavily involved in banking — and indeed mergers between banks and brokers are increasing at a fast pace.

The insurance industry is not immune to this homogenization. Increasingly, insurance products have the look and feel of investable instruments. This is certainly true of annuities and to a lesser extent life insurance.

With so many lines blurring between financial products, it may even be hard to make a distinction between what is a securities product and what is life-insurance oriented. A basic rule of thumb, for the moment anyway, is that life insurance products tend to give investors the potential of a large payoff after a grace period. This is slightly different than an investment in, say, equities or fixed income instruments where the payoff is more liquid — and the investment may accrue profit on a monthly, weekly or even daily basis.

Annuities: Unlike plain-vanilla stock investments, annuities demand an initial and ongoing investment in return for tax-advantaged withdrawals at a later date. An investor who seeks to remove his or her capital before the appointed time will find that it is subject to withdrawal penalties.

Annuities gained favor in the 1990s as computers allowed insurance firms to create increasingly flexible products featuring these tax-advantaged instruments. Variable annuities which place an investor's capital in equities with virtually unlimited upside — while giving the investor some assurance his or her principal will be preserved — proved increasingly popular through the 1990s. Variable annuity contracts and their underlying subaccounts are subject to market risk which causes their value to fluctuate.

Throughout the 20th century, products were defined by the industry that offered them. Insurers offered life insurance, banks offered CDs and Wall Street broker-dealers offered stocks and bonds. In the future, as computers break down these differences, instruments will be differentiated by the markets they represent rather than the industry that offer them. It is already fashionable to point out that investors can make returns similar to that offered by annuities if they simply save and invest in a disciplined fashion. The key word here, however, is discipline. The value of financial products such as annuities may eventually be seen in terms of the savings discipline they enforce rather than the specific investment opportunities they offer.

Insurance: The same may be said (to a lesser degree) for life insurance. Investors may use a variety of vehicles to build limited nest eggs to care for loved ones in case of their untimely demise. In fact, the array of annuities and life insurance products is increasingly complicated. As domestic tax laws interact with such products in increasingly complex ways, some insurance agents have taken to selling life insurance policies as a way to aid estate planning.

Term insurance: This type of insurance provides the greatest death benefit for the lowest cost. Term insurance is generally best suited for short-term needs or situations where the affordability of insurance is severely hampered. The easiest way to understand term insurance is to compare it to automobile insurance. When you buy automobile insurance, you pay a fixed premium for a fixed term. If you don't get into a car accident, you don't collect on the insurance. When your automobile insurance comes up for renewal, your premiums generally rise.

Term insurance works the same way. You make your premium payments. If you don't die, you do not get anything back. Similar to automobile insurance, term insurance premiums go up every year. This is because the chances of you dying increases each and every year. Statistics show that very few term insurance policies ever pay a death benefit. This is because many older policyholders do not renew their policies because the premiums grow too large.

Whole life insurance: Another name for whole life insurance is permanent insurance. This type of insurance is permanent in nature. The premiums remain fixed throughout the lifetime of the insured. In addition to the death benefit, whole life insurance contains a cash value feature that provides the insured with a living benefit as well. Because of this added feature, premiums for whole life insurance policies are higher than those for term insurance.

These independent advisors offer clients fee-based financial advice. The advisor works with the client to write and implement an investment policy statement. But the main reason to use a financial advisor is to get financial options.

For example, a 30 year old man buys a whole life

insurance policy. Let's assume a premium of $1,000 a year. When this man reaches 40 years old, his premium will still be $1,000. If this 30 year old man bought a term life insurance policy, his initial premium may be $200 per year, but as he approaches 40, the premium will often rise each every year.

Universal life insurance: Universal life insurance contains features of both term insurance and whole life insurance. It is similar to term insurance in that premiums are based on the client's current age. It is similar to whole life insurance in that the policy builds cash value. Think of universal life insurance as a savings account that pays life insurance premiums. For example, let's assume that the client buys a universal life insurance policy with a premium of $1,000 per year. Let's also assume that the cost of insuring this client is $400 per year. The insurance company will remove $400 out of the client's cash account to pay for the death benefit and leave the remaining $600 to earn interest.

Another name for universal life insurance is flexible premium life insurance. This is because the client has enormous flexibility in funding the plan. As long as there is enough money in the cash account for the life insurance company to withdraw the death benefit cost, the client need not pay any premiums. Returning to our example above, if the client has $600 remaining in his cash account earning interest, and the next year's death benefit cost is $400, there is no need for the client to make a premium payment for that year. However, in the following year, if the cost of the death benefit exceeds the amount of money in the savings account, the client will get a notice from the insurance company to replenish the cash account.

Competition has increased in the life insurance business, with more and more companies offering products to the public such as variable life and variable universal life. These policies are similar to the whole life insurance and universal life insurance mentioned above, in that they build cash value. They are different from the policies mentioned above in that the cash values are not guaranteed; the amount of cash value that is accumulated is directly related to the performance of equity-based investment components of the policy.

Investors who have read this far may want to find some professional help when sorting through the complex menu of financial products that can aid in retirement and estate planning, in addition to buttressing an ongoing investment plan. These days, the fastest growing segment of financial consulting is on the independent side.

Planners & consultants: Just as computers are changing the face of finance, so they are changing how financial advice is delivered. It used to be that brokers sold stock, life insurance agents sold insurance and bankers offered loans and home mortgages. These days, thanks to the computer and the ability of financial advisors to use software programs to coherently organize a client's financial situation, a whole industry comprised of independent financial planners has begun offering their services to a clientele of wealthy and middle-income families.

These independent advisors offer clients fee-based financial advice. The advisor works with the client to write and implement an investment policy statement. But the main reason to use a financial advisor is to get a sense of the financial options available and to insure that these options are evaluated and that a plan is put into place that allows for the disciplined accrual of assets according to the agreed-on strategy.

The advantages of using an outside advisor include:

Time savings: Time has become a scarce resource in today's rapid-paced world. Few people have enough time to do all the things they want to do. An advisor can free you from the responsibility of drafting your investment policy statement, implementing it, and reviewing your portfolio on a quarterly basis.

Discipline: Money is a very emotional subject for most people. It can be hard to make emotionally detached, rational decisions regarding one's own money. A financial advisor can solve this problem by bringing objectivity to financial decision-making.

Knowledge: Most individual investors do not have the training required to be effective investors on their own. Gathering this knowledge and staying up to date is time-consuming and costly. Few investors are willing to make this kind of commitment.

A good financial advisor can have a significant impact on your investment success. Let's look at one study completed by Dalbar Financial Services, Inc., to see how much value an advisor can add. This study shows the total returns earned by individual investors who invested on their own using directly marketed investment products, compared with those who worked with a financial advisor. The results: From January 1984 through September 1993, investors using a financial advisor realized total returns of 90.21% versus 70.23% for the do-it-yourself investors.

27

SECTION SUMMARY

Educated Investors understand what fuels the investment engine at home and abroad. By better understanding its component parts — its various instruments and strategies — investors can build portfolios that most efficiently make use of available monetary fuel. These include:

- Equity, issued in its simplest form as stock in various corporate efforts to fulfill business purposes.
- Fixed income, offered in various forms with various maturities to investors who are willing to lend money to the issuer in return for interest payments and assurance that the principal will be returned at the end of the lending cycle.
- Tangible assets, available to investors who understand that the business cycle both inflates and deflates securitized assets and thus wish to hold assets that may be less susceptible to monetary swings.
- Money strategies developed by money managers making use of the computer to blend equity, fixed-income and even tangible assets, generating various forms of hedged, international exposure.
- IPOs, small stocks and derivatives — instruments that Educated Investors may not find immediately applicable to the creation of diversified portfolios but that are, nonetheless, potentially part of a broad investment arsenal.
- Annuities, insurance and planning — various strategies that may be suggested by qualified financial advisors as part of an overall financial plan.

FOUR

21ST CENTURY INVESTING

28

FUTURE OF MARKET STRUCTURE

WHAT EDUCATED INVESTORS UNDERSTAND ABOUT MARKETS' EVOLUTION

Educated Investors understand that the computer is changing the way the financial industry operates. They know the neat packages of 20th century regulation are about to give way, and that the 21st century is ushering in a great change in how markets function and individuals purchase and trade securities.

By anticipating such changes, Educated Investors make investing easier and less surprising. Knowledge adds confidence. Understanding how markets are evolving gives Educated Investors more control over their own destiny, economic and otherwise. An investor who is less fearful and more educated is an investor who will be less prone to the mistakes panic can induce.

But where exactly are 21st century markets headed? First of all, it is important to understand that large markets already don't differentiate enormously between products. Stocks, bonds and other forms of underlying securitized instruments are increasingly mixed, matched and bundled. The overarching consideration when trading such instruments has to do with interest rates and economic conditions. Many of these considerations, given the bigness of these bets, are macro in nature. And the markets in which these billion-dollar swaps and derivative products are traded is increasingly large as well. What is emerging in the computerized, post-20th century trading environment is an increasingly cohesive electronic marketplace put in place between the largest corporate, institutional and banking players.

This is the opinion of California-based financial futurist Peter Schwartz among others. Schwartz thinks that what may emerge worldwide over the next decade or two is some kind of two-tier market that would consist of a relatively unregulated group of perhaps 100 to 1,000 transition or global companies involved in international trading and underwriting. This international tier will evolve on top of a regionalized market structure. In such an environment, it's possible that the biggest players would serve as their own regulatory agents and provide their own free-floating exchange nets. In fact, this is what's happening even now as the world's biggest banks and institutions trade a slew of virtually unregulated securitized products, most of which have been enhanced and bundled by the application of computer power to the underlying instrument.

A couple of things are quite fundamental in shaping the future of the markets, Schwartz points out. The first is the increasing rapidity and size of capital flows; the second is the ability to integrate and operate our evolving automated markets; and the third is the eventual stratification of the marketplace.

"The bulk of international global trading is inefficient and unobserved," Schwartz says. "It ripples into our domestic market in ways we often choose to deny. What we're going to get, probably in a piecemeal fashion, is a market for consenting adults with more than $100 million to invest, who have the sophistication and systems to trade in the global arena. These adult players will trade in an environment with a minimum of rules where the biggest risks are counterparty risks — 'Can I

A couple of things are quite fundamental in shaping the future of the markets, Schwartz points out. The first is the increasing rapidity and size of capital flows; the second is the ability to integrate and operate automated markets.

trust the guy on the other side to honor his commitment?' "

Schwartz' vision of the financial marketplace is probably an accurate one. However, such analysis usually glosses over the inevitable difficulties that change engenders. It has been pointed out, for instance, that with the increasing emphasis on international electronic trading of customized instruments — derivatives — that allow institutions to create securitized assets with tremendous leverage, institutions are taking on commitments far beyond their asset bases. The actual amount of borrowing that the United States' largest money-center banks have undertaken in the 1990s is in the area of $15-$20 trillion. This is far more than the total amount of assets on hand.

A negative market event, say worried financial observers, could have potentially disastrous consequences for the world's largest monetary players. The result would be bankruptcy, failure and increased inflation. Worst case, the world's largest financial institutions would suffer through a difficult and chaotic time. There would be calls for change, even for the banning of computerized finance. This is simply not going to happen. The computer is a tool. And tools will be used.

Educated Investors who understand how markets are evolving worldwide, what the dangers are and what scenarios may take place, will be in a better position to tend to their own finances bereft of misunderstandings about how the money business really works. Having anticipated what can go wrong, they will not be surprised if it does. Instead, having a basic understanding of these issues, they will cope.

As *Economist* contributor Rupert Pennant-Rea has pointed out, "Finance is about risk, and there are no ways of making a risky business risk-free." However, domestic and international regulators should take a step back from rulemaking, Pennant-Rea adds, and help business organize its transborder finances more rationally through electronic exchange mechanisms.

According to such financial futurists, what is needed today is a process similar to what the United States went through in the late 1800s when it finally began to establish a true national economy.

The danger, say these futurists, is that regulatory obstruction will make this evolution more difficult and retard capital flows. Efficient, automated systems for executing and settling the trade will be of high value. The world's biggest financial institutions won't wish to be constrained by boundaries. "They'll want efficiency," says Schwartz — a minimum of rules and a maximum of efficiency.

And he adds, "All this has tremendous implications. For one thing, we'll have to stop thinking of companies as domestic or foreign. Countries will begin to attract surges of capital from huge private entities instead of depending on handouts from world organizations."

Bigness is not by itself something that markets and democracies ought to fear. But bigness mandated by government, and supported by regulation and federally-granted monopolies is another matter. Educated Investors will watch for such trends and draw their own conclusions.

29

FUTURE OF REGULATION

WHAT EDUCATED INVESTORS UNDERSTAND ABOUT REGULATORY EVOLUTION

Educated Investors know that their best defense against financial fraud and market volatility is an understanding of how markets work, what Modern Portfolio Theory suggests about investing and where to go to obtain valid investment-oriented information.

Despite all the good intentions of our political leaders on federal, state and local levels, Educated Investors are well aware that financial regulation is not a panacea and will not compensate for foolishness.

Educated Investors are also aware — as this book has discussed — that computer power is changing the way the financial industry operates, the way investment products are generated and offered and the way that institutions with access to the most complex and powerful financial software and hardware can react to trends much more quickly than the average investor. Thus, in the 21st century, computer power and access to sophisticated financial information will become a key to investment success.

Educated Investors know that the domestic regulatory apparatus, at least on a Federal level, is not set up for purposes of protection so much as for purposes of information dissemination. As state regulators like Colorado's Lee Poulson have pointed out, the Securities and Exchange Commission, from its very inception, has observed a mandate to withhold judgments about the prospects of an offering or new securities instrument.

So long as information is properly and legally presented in a prospectus, the Securities and Exchange Commission will pass on that registration and allow the issue to become public.

Additionally, as technology continues to reconfigure how financial markets evolve, Educated Investors will watch for signs that the regulatory apparatus is evolving too.

Educated Investors are well aware that 21st century market regulation must be flexible. Regulation must deal with issues of solvency and imaginative decentralization brought on by an increasingly electronic financial industry.

Educated Investors look for three regulatory trends that will make markets stronger and broader in the 21 century.

Industry participation: Healthy 21st century regulation will be about encouraging larger financial players to set up their own industry-driven structures. This self-regulatory model has been applied in the U.S. through this country's "self-regulatory organizations" such as the New York Stock Exchange and the National Association of Securities dealers. It is the industry itself which can best monitor leverage, encourage fiscal responsibility and weed out irresponsible participants.

Competition: This can be stimulated through creative regulation, forcing institutions, despite their discomfort, to engage in creative thinking about ways to structure their investment programs.

Information: Another healthy kind of regulatory strate-

Competition can be stimulated through creative regulation forcing institutions to engage in creative thinking about ways to structure their investment programs.

gy is one that encourages "sunshine" — the use of the various electronic systems now coming onto the market to disseminate increased amounts of market information.

Educated Investors will monitor the progress of regulation in the 21st century and make adjustments to their portfolios and expectations as the situation warrants.

30

FUTURE OF MONEY

WHAT EDUCATED INVESTORS UNDERSTAND ABOUT MONETARY EVOLUTION

The easiest change to predict when it comes to money is one that is both cosmetic and fundamental. The future of money is now fairly well mapped-out. It will, more and more, be a future that includes plastic-embedded microchips that transmit information about our solvency and net worth.

These so-called "omni-cards" will be useful almost anywhere in more technologically proficient societies. This does not mean that cash — paper money — will be phased out altogether, but that more and more people will find great convenience in using omni-cards with their credit, debt and cash features available in one place.

How will this work? Using a cash omni-card feature, someone might buy a soda from a soda machine. Using an electronic credit-line feature, someone might purchase a car. Using the card's electronic debt feature — electronic information on how much money is in an available savings or checking account — someone might buy furniture or a gift via the Internet or physically at a department store.

To support these omni cards, government and private industry will set up huge electronic clearinghouses. These clearinghouses will be developed by the world's largest banks and will contain a myriad of electronic information about a person's financial life and perhaps even a number of other details such as a person's health and social history including criminal records and employment history.

Perhaps all of this sounds a little like a Big Brother scenario — a point that has some people worried. Certainly it cannot be denied that the power of the omni-card when combined with the power of instantly accessible computer information will be an awesome social tool for good or ill. And chances are that power will be used for both — though hopefully more for good than bad.

Educated Investors, aware of the coming electronic age of money will be both wary about its potential negative consequences and eager to participate in the elements that make life easier — whether these have to do with online investing and banking or increased shopping opportunities via the Internet. Opportunities made more viable because of omni-card availability.

Money will not just change its shape and substance. Money will also change in terms of currency. Chances are, as debt, credit and cash features converge, so will the world's currencies begin to converge. This is already happening as more and more countries adopt so-called currency boards in which these countries participating central banks pin their own currency's value to the value of the dollar.

The power of the omni-card when combined with the power of instant computer information will be an awesome social tool for good or ill. And chances are that this power will be used for both — though hopefully more for good.

Additionally, Europe's central banks are moving toward creating the so-called euro that will eventually replace Europe's many competing currencies.

It is probably safe to say that the 21st century will see fewer kinds of currencies and a consolidated type of money material (omni-card) that will allow users increased credit flexibility.

The convenience and power of this scenario cannot be denied. Nor can the impetus toward centralization of information, credit and monetary policy. And therein lies the rub. Like everything else having to do with money, such centralization carries with it benefits and risks. Educated Investors, aware of this fundamental point, will not simply be cheerleaders for this electronic evolution. They will be well aware of the risks that are inherent in this kind of centralization, the bureaucracies that can be created and the capacity that this kind of centralization has for misuse and even abuse.

Even as Educated Investors take advantage of the many conveniences that electronic money will certainly bring, these leaders will continue to examine alternatives that electronic money offers via the Internet through private monetary efforts. Already on the Internet there are many ways to link one's savings directly to an underlying money guarantee such as gold.

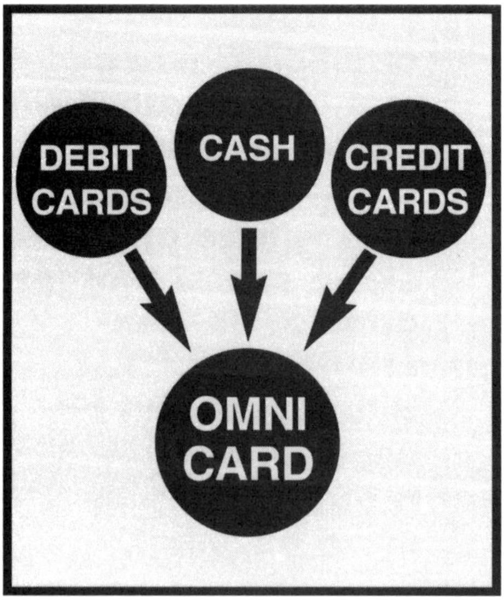

Ultimately money is credit. As this credit becomes more or less a function of electronic messages, people's lives will be enriched by the convenience inherent in electronic communication. At the same time, privacy risks and risks to one's financial and personal freedoms will surely increase. For this reason, Educated Investors will adopt the same stance that they have adopted when it comes to other investment evolutions — they will closely monitor this paperless revolution, try to enhance their own personal wealth and wellbeing by applying its positive aspects and take care to avoid the negative ones whenever possible.

31

INVEST, DON'T SPECULATE

SPECULATORS MAKE BETS, BUT EDUCATED INVESTORS DON'T NEED TO

Speculators may have a system, even a discipline, but they have no assurance as to whether they will win or lose. An investor has an understanding gained through serious, disciplined study.

A speculator guesses. An investor knows.

In the last three chapters we have examined the future of markets, financial regulation and money. Throughout this book, we have examined how our financial system evolved and changed to get to its present point.

In this final chapter we will sum up what we have covered — what's necessary to be an Educated Investor.

To begin with, we examined the three principles of finance. We learned that investing could not take place in countries and regions where the right of property was not respected. We learned that business cycles exist and that Educated Investors follow them and learn from them. Finally, we learned that allocating assets using the discipline of Modern Portfolio Theory is a fundamental part of being an Educated Investor.

We also learned about different instruments and how they could be used by Educated Investors to create balanced portfolios. Finally, we learned about the future of finance, including the direction of markets, regulation and money.

In the rest of this chapter, we will discuss in more detail the evolution of money. This may sound odd since the last chapter was on this same subject. But there is still more to say — enough so that it deserves a special place at the end of this book.

It is important to have another discussion of money because we have not yet discussed its fundamental nature.

Articles have been appearing with greater or lesser validity in major periodicals like *Time* magazine about the nature of money for the last few years. These articles tend to discuss money much as the last chapter of this book discussed it — in terms of how it will look and how people will use it in the 21st century.

But the fundamental nature of money does not have much to do with its use nor with its appearance.

Money has intrinsic value. It's that simple.

Throughout the ages, intrinsic value has resided in numerous items — shells, beads, metals and, of course, the most common money-metal, gold.

Gold, as famous scholars have pointed out, became the money metal of choice through a market competition of over 5,000 years.

As money evolved, various representative substances were created that extended the value of gold since gold was not easily transported or traded. Chief among these substances were coins and bills — usually paper bills.

For the first 200 years of this country's existence, paper bills were issued by banks and other entities (even restaurants and saloons) that were convertible to gold. But in this century — in this country and throughout the world — the printing and disseminating of money became the job of the Federal government. With the dissolution of a 1940s treaty called Bretton-Woods, the American dollar and other currencies throughout the world were formally delinked from gold. That "barbarous relic" — as famous economist John Maynard Keynes called it — was removed from the monetary scene as a repository of value. Today, the only place that gold is a recognized monetary store of

> **Educated Investors understand what fuels the investment engine at home and abroad. By better understanding its component parts — its various instruments and strategies — investors can build better and more efficient portfolios.**

value is in the vaults of central banks (an ironic situation according to some).

In any event, the 20th century seems to have seen a fundamental shift away from the everyday use of gold as a trading mechanism. Instead of gold, most people associate money with the power of their democratic government — the "full faith and credit" of government has replaced gold as money's surety. This would seem to be a fundamental shift in the way money is viewed and used.

Democracies are quite wonderful things in that everyone can have a voice and the most powerful interest groups can make the biggest changes. This encourages compromise and evolutionary, rather than revolutionary, change. The trouble with democracies, especially when the power to create money is in the hands of elected officials and cooperative banking groups, is that these officials will often try to expand the money supply too fast in an attempt to satisfy everybody. It is this expansion of the money supply that creates credit and ultimately inflation.

This credit and money inflation can also cause things like stock market bubbles. As credit expands, and then contracts, it causes what we know as a business cycle.

Educated Investors understand this business cycle and they also understand the fundamental rules governing money have not changed. When there is too much money — when officials and bankers in trying to please their constituencies have made too much credit and paper money available — then the money and goods created by that abundant supply becomes less valuable.

Tell someone that he or she will not use paper dollar bills in the future but will use instead an omni-card, and they will soon begin to engage you in a spirited conversation. They may agree or disagree, but they will certainly have an opinion. It is more difficult, in the current day, to engage people in a conversation about the underlying, intrinsic value of money. Though it is important, it is as natural to most people as breathing. They don't question it. Thus they don't think about it and have a difficult time talking about it. Yet it is this discussion, this knowledge, that builds truly Educated Investors.

These Educated Investors understand not only the causes of the business cycle, they never forget that the true nature of money probably won't change as much as people think it will over the next 100 years.

In fact, it probably won't change at all. It may look different, but ultimately, it will act in much the same way as it always has. When there is too much of it around, it will be worth less, regardless of whether its intrinsic value is stored in an omni-card or a dollar bill.

When it is worth more, people will feel happy and confident. When it is worth less, people will notice that their hard work doesn't seem to buy as much as it used to.

Inflation, in the 20th century, as in the 19th century and 18th century and every century preceding that, is a monetary phenomenon. So long as money and credit are available through democratic processes supervised by elected officials and bankers, the temptation will be to overexpand the money supply.

The simplest way to think of this is to remember that when there was too much gold in circulation, people would simply stop digging it out of the ground. The price of gold would soon stabilize. If there were too little of it, people would find more. When the responsibility for putting money and credit into circulation becomes the responsibility of elected officials, the discipline the market exerts over the money supply may be diminished.

Famous monetarists like Milton Friedman say that elected officials and central bankers can put discipline back into the process of printing money and issuing credit by using the free market as their guide. But this still leaves it up to individuals responsible for monetary policy to determine what the market is telling them. Sometimes these people will recognize the right signs and sometimes they won't. In any event, in a democracy it is very difficult to reduce the money supply since that reduction tends to cause a recession — and people don't like recessions.

If there is one thing that Educated Investors understand, it is the above evolution of money and the business cycle that is caused by credit expansion and contraction.

It is only by being very aware of these cycles — and some of them can last as long as 25-50 years (or most of a person's lifetime) — that an Educated Investor can position his or her assets and invest judiciously.

Too often, the noise of the crowd — TV, newspapers and magazines — becomes a distraction and conflicting advice leads to confusion. By simplifying investing and keeping the fundamental nature of money in mind, Educated Investors see more clearly than others how markets react and how business cycles change.

Each investor has a unique risk-tolerance level. Your risk tolerance can be characterized by the amount of short-term loss you are willing to accept in order to achieve your long-term goals. You should not take greater risk than you are comfortable with; taking such risk is the surest road to financial failure.

If there is a market downturn, and you are taking too much risk, you might panic and sell your positions. However, if you design your portfolio with your risk tolerance in mind, you will be able to ride out a downturn and achieve investment success. If you are like most investors, you want the highest return possible.

The challenge every investor faces in the quest for return enhancement is to resist getting caught up in the advice given in the numerous financial magazines and investment newsletter publications that play on our emotions; and this advice is often fraught with contradictory indications.

In monetary terms, change is contained. Given current government policies, there are only two choices, actually: reflation and deflation (or their subsets, inflation and disinflation).

In the case of real-money deflation, cash is certainly king. First of all, paper money, the dollar, becomes the repository of increasing value — then perhaps foreign currencies, or even precious metals, as confidence erodes. Real estate, securities, and other asset-based investments become devalued in a deflation.

In a reflation, things are perhaps easier to predict, at least on a macro-level. Tangible assets are a store of increasing value; commodities, real estate, and inflation-resistant securities are all good choices. Investors, however, must pay their money and take their chances.

Educated Investors who do not want to choose will diversify broadly beyond stocks and bonds, keeping some assets in gold or money markets, as well as in low-fee principal-guaranteed managed futures funds if investors can find good ones. They will hope that whatever happens does not so overwhelm any one sector of the market as to render a swath of their portfolio worthless.

A very simple fail-safe plan divides assets into thirds: a third in equities, a third in gold, and a third in reserves with rebalancing annually. This strategy will protect in both a low- and high-interest rate environment.

Educated Investors seek to understand financial markets and business cycles and where our financial system —

worldwide — is headed. Familiar with Modern Portfolio Theory and the organization of our current monetary system, Educated Investors will invest in a cautious but disciplined fashion — bearing in mind the current stage of the business cycle and the nature of the fund or instrument in which they are placing assets.

Asset allocation, a long-term, disciplined approach to investing and a healthy respect for the unpredictability of markets and instruments — in an increasingly leveraged and computerized economic environment — are some keys Educated Investors use to unlock wealth for themselves and their loved ones.

Investing isn't easy. Neither is education. There are few truly Educated Investors. Will you be one of them?

32

SECTION SUMMARY & CONCLUSION

Educated Investors never stop learning. They realize education is not static — it's a state of becoming, not a state of being.

Educated Investors, having internalized basic tenets of monetary history, watch carefully to see how financial trends may have a direct or indirect effect on the future of finance. Educated Investors analyze and track:

• Market structure, observing how markets are expanding and gradually generating, worldwide, an electronic two-tiered market structure of larger and smaller participants.

• Financial regulation, noticing how it applies to the modern, computerized markets of the 21 century, how it may be reconfigured and what impact it will have on a broadly traded, electronic market made up of fairly uncategorizeable financial instruments.

• Money, discerning how changes in the way various repositories of value are traded or produced affect the underlying monetary engine — its generation and dispersal of credit.

•

Educated Investors may well be proponents of the financial and monetary system as it is, observing that its regulated, yet broad-based, benefits have increasingly allowed countries and economies around the world to participate in the benefits of modern agriculture, medicine and science.

These investors may note that the system has been gathering strength since the Industrial Revolution and despite fairly bloody interludes of 20th century despotism, they may look with approval at its increasing ascendancy at the end of the 20th.

Doubtless there is much to take issue with in the way monetary policy is orchestrated and offered both domestically and throughout the world. And as this monetary policy is increasingly consolidated through various monetary unions, there will be more debate over its configuration and impact. But Educated Investors also know that policy concerns and real-life investing are separate issues. No matter what occurs in the first years of the 21st century, Educated Investors will keep in mind certain fundamental truths — the truths that separate Educated Investors from the uneducated.

Let's review them here.

Educated Investors — whether professional money managers or informed individuals — build strong portfolios using:

- Free markets.
- Knowledge of what constitutes business cycles.
- Knowledge of Modern Portfolio Theory to generate asset-allocation strategies that react to or anticipate the domestic or international business cycles.

Educated Investors — whether professional money managers or informed individuals — make a commitment to understanding:

- The difference between business cycles and market volatility.
- How Wall Street works and why structure is less important than monetary policy.
- The ramifications of taxes and the process — and effect — of market and investment regulation.
- The truth about international investing and why too much "noise" can often prejudice otherwise sound investment decisions.

Educated Investors understand what fuels the investment engine at home and abroad. By better understanding its component parts — its various instruments and strategies — investors can build portfolios that most efficiently make use of available monetary fuel. These include:

- Equity, issued in its simplest form as stock in various corporate efforts to fulfill business purposes.

• Fixed income, offered in various forms with various maturities to investors who are willing to lend money to the issuer in return for interest payments and assurance that the principal will be returned at the end of the lending cycle.

• Tangible assets, available to investors who understand that the business cycle both inflates and deflates securitized assets and thus wish to hold assets that may be less susceptible to monetary swings.

• Money strategies developed by money managers making use of the computer to blend equity, fixed-income and even tangible assets generating various forms of hedged international exposure.

• IPOs, small stocks and derivatives — instruments that Educated Investors may not find immediately applicable to the creation of diversified portfolios but that are, nonetheless, potentially part of a broad investment arsenal.

• Annuities, insurance and planning — various strategies that may be suggested by qualified financial advisors as part of an overall financial plan.

Educated Investors will keep in mind that the use of the above instruments, in any combination, should only be undertaken with due consideration and after considerable discussion with trusted advisors including a qualified financial advisor or planner.

Educated Investors understand what fuels the investment engine at home and abroad. By better understanding its component parts — its various instruments and strategies — investors can build better and more efficient portfolios.

It is important to emphasize that those who adopt all the conclusions of Modern Portfolio Theory will take a very disciplined approach to investing, use asset-allocation funds and reallocation models beyond the scope of this book.

For those who continue to feel that investing contains an element of art, a knowledge and respect for Modern Portfolio Theory's findings are to be combined with a more intuitive approach that features real-life experience and a willingness to go beyond models and statistics.

Remember, the Educated Investor is a slave to neither fashion nor dogma. As reality reconfigures investment verities, as new research confirms or disproves various investment methodologies, the Educated Investor will take note and adapt his or her financial — and intellectual — position accordingly.

Educated Investing is an exciting, challenging and disciplined process. If you have read this far, you are well on your way to becoming part of it.

Good luck as you set forth on the path to Educated Investing.

May you never reach its end!

GLOSSARY OF USEFUL TERMS

ACTIVE MONEY MANAGER: (vs. passive) manager who chooses securities by pulling together a variety of fundamental and economic data.

ASSET: something that can be bought or sold.

BOND: corporate, government, municipal security that offers regular interest to investors as well as final payment. Bondholders have no corporate ownership privileges; stockholders do.

BROKER: a securities salesperson employed by a firm to sell financial products, usually for a percentage of the commission.

BROKER-DEALER: a broker acts as intermediary between buyer and seller. Dealer buys and sells for own account and also underwrites securities.

CALLS: in options, the ability to purchase, on a certain date or dates, certain security or securities at a specified price.

CASH SETTLEMENT: cash received for the market value of an instrument at a certain point in time. Often refers to the futures or options markets where instruments settle monthly or quarterly at face value.

CLOSED-END FUND: a fund, typically listed on an exchange, often composed of securities whose total value is more than the actual price at which the fund's shares are trading. Since closed-end fund managers have no obligation to redeem shares at net asset value, fund participants are often forced to sell for less than their shares are actually worth.

COMMERCIAL BANK: bank that takes deposits and makes loans in addition to private placement business. As opposed to a merchant bank, which places its own capital at risk in private deals, and an investment bank, which places its capital at risk in underwriting public issues.

COMMODITIES FUTURES TRADING COMMISSION (CFTC): established in 1974, after SEC turned down responsibility; regulates commodities and financial futures. Oversight includes fair practice, disclosure, and maintenance of orderly markets.

COMMODITY: goods of a nonfinancial nature such as grain or metals, often traded on a futures exchange.

DEBT: longer-term fixed income securities (see bond).

DERIVATIVE(S): securities whose worth is based on an underlying instrument. Prices of options and financial futures, for instance, have some connection to the movements of underlying equity. But many derivatives are traded off-exchange; their popularity is growing along with questions about how well Wall Street actually understands the risks inherent in these OTC customized instruments.

DIVIDEND: shareholder profits on company earnings, often distributed quarterly.

DOW JONES INDUSTRIAL AVERAGE: thirty big NYSE-traded stocks whose average is presumably representative of the market as a whole; price-weighted.

EQUITY: in industry terminology, a fancy word for stocks.

EXCHANGE: used to be a building, owned or rented by members, where securities were traded. Now can refer to an electronic net.

EXECUTION: buying or selling of a security.

FAIR MARKET: one offering the buyer the lowest possible price and the seller the highest possible one in comparison to similar markets.

FINANCIAL FUTURE: futures contract including those based on underlying instruments such as long bonds, mortgages or stock indexes.

FIXED INCOME: (see bond.)

GLASS-STEAGALL: this 1934 Act separated private banking functions from public dealing and brokering functions.

Henceforth, banks could not underwrite securities, nor recommend their sale. Today banks can underwrite corporate debt and even, in some cases, launch stock offerings. Glass-Steagall is tottering.

INDEX ARBITRAGE: the process of buying in one market while simultaneously selling in another.

INITIAL PUBLIC OFFERING (IPO): the first offering of stock to the public.

INSTITUTION: any large financial management entity not identified with Wall Street's "sell side."

INTEREST RATE: the expense of using borrowed cash or securities.

LIMITED PARTNER: investor in public or private partnership.

LIMITED PARTNERSHIP: these come in two flavors, public and private. Private partnerships are restricted to 100 partners or less, along with a general partner or partners; public partnerships may have thousands of investors, usually at $5,000 per, along with a general partner or partners.

LIQUIDITY: the ability of a market to quickly accommodate the buyer and seller at an acceptable price.

M&A: stands for mergers and acquisitions.

MARKET IMPACT: the purchase or sale of a security in such a way that it moves the market as it changes hands.

MARKET-MAKERS: In NASD terminology, are those traders who stand ready to buy or sell securities for their own account. Unlike specialist systems, more than one market maker may have responsibility to insure an orderly market in a given stock.

MONEY MANAGER: term commonly used to refer to someone who runs portfolios professionally for an institutional fund or pension plan.

MUTUAL FUND: these are funds, open or closed-end, that operate under the rules of the 1940 Investment Company Act, which mandates disclosure of performance and investment objectives.

NASD: National Association of Securities Dealers, a self-regulatory organization set up by the SEC and the Investment Bankers' Conference to regulate the myriad OTC firms of the 1 930s across the country. One goal: "to establish high moral and ethical standards in securities trading." Association later developed an electronic trading net, Nasdaq.

PORTFOLIO: more than a single security under management or owned by an individual or group.

PROSPECTUS: a written explanation of securities being offered.

PUT (OPTIONS): the ability to sell, at a certain price, at a certain time, a specific number of securities.

QUOTES: offers to buy or sell securities.

REAL ESTATE INVESTMENT TRUSTS (REITS): a company overseeing a real estate portfolio for shareholders and passing along profits, if any.

SECURITIES EXCHANGE COMMISSION (SEC): created by the Securities and Exchange Act of 1934 to administer that act and supervise the implementation of the rules of the Securities Act of 1933. The SEC is responsible for supervising statutes promoting full public disclosure and for protecting the public against securities fraud. The SEC supervises exchanges and investment companies, advisers, and the NASD.

SECONDARY MARKET: the physical or automated market venue in which financial instruments are bought and sold.

SECURITY(IES): bonds, stocks, other kinds of financial instruments, offered publicly or privately.

SETTLEMENT: the process of settling a trade; i.e., taking in the cash on one side and delivering the security on the other.

STOCK: ownership in a corporation.

TREASURY (TREASURYS): government bonds.

UNDERWRITING: the process of purchasing securities from an issuer with the intent of selling them soon; a function commonly performed by Wall Street's banking firms.